What People Are Saying about
Chris Dupré and *Unstuck*...

"*Unstuck*! What a great title and what a great book! As a pastor and leader I've seen countless people who for one reason or another have become "stuck." Chris DuPré's book, *Unstuck*, not only goes to the heart of why so many people can't move forward, it gives voice to the struggle as well as hope for the heart. Chris has been a dear friend for over twenty-five years. I've seen him wrestle with things that others might use as an excuse to remain stuck, and yet he found in God what was needed to triumph and to move on to what God had next for him and for his family. Chris' pastoral heart and insight come out so clearly in his latest book. I recommend *Unstuck* to anyone needing wisdom, vision, and hope on this journey called life."

—*Mike Bickle*
Director, International House of Prayer
Kansas City, MO

"Chris DuPré has written a deeply powerful work inspired by the Holy Spirit that sets people free. It is one of those books that we need to read over and over and let the words sink in deeply to our hearts to bring change and healing in our lives. I love it!"

—*Dr. Cindy Jacobs*
Generals International

Richest Blessings

Chris DuPré

John 8:36

"It is remarkable that as a generation with unprecedented opportunities, so many of us have believed the lie that we simply "can't." However, the Word of God never returns void. (See Isaiah 55:11.) *Unstuck* is a wonderful reminder of the promises of Jeremiah 29:11—that the Lord has plans and purposes for our future, which will be fulfilled if we persevere. Our Father says that we *can*! We just need to hold on to hope, by faith and patience, and press through the hurdles that try to hinder us. Knowing our identity as overcomers in Christ, we inherit the promises. Through his personal stories and anecdotes, Chris DuPré exhorts us that it *is* possible to break through the facades of fear, rejection, delay, intimidation by the unknown, and more. *Unstuck* is a gift to believers in all seasons of life, inspiring them to *believe* again that though we may face challenges and feel knocked down, as the righteous, we get back up, seven times over! (See Proverbs 24:16.)"

—*Dr. Ché Ahn*
President, Harvest International Ministry
Founding Pastor, HROCK Church, Pasadena, CA
International Chancellor, Wagner University

"Perhaps you have wondered why you are not more highly motivated or why you don't go for greater fulfillment in life. Can this be changed? Yes! *Unstuck* by Chris DuPré will help you! Chris explains how beliefs held in the heart such as fear, rejection, and pride, act like quicksand, keeping us from rising to our potential. Discouragement sets in, and we back off. But if you honestly face your issues, you can get unstuck and go for your dreams. Well done, Chris; the nation and the world need this message desperately."

—*John Arnott*
Catch the Fire/Partners in Harvest
Toronto, Canada

"When Jesus was asked questions concerning the issues of life, He would often tell stories. Some of those stories are called parables—real or fictional illustrations with applications for understanding life and how things really work. Similarly, Chris DuPré, a collector of wisdom and a master storyteller, has packed the pages of *Unstuck* with real-life experience and insight. He writes with delightful transparency that makes wisdom easy to find. This is a book to read and share. If you don't need 'unsticking,' then surely your friends and family do!"

—*Charles Stock*
Senior pastor, Life Center, Harrisburg, PA
Founder, Clear River Network

"Is there something holding you back? Is there an impossibility in front of you today? Here's the way out—the way to be *unstuck*. Chris DuPré has given you an amazing toolbox of revelation to set you free from any and every disappointment life could throw at you. With an amazing flair for communicating, Chris presents truths that will keep you thinking for days after you have finished reading it. I loved hearing him share so candidly about his life journey—a journey that hasn't always been a piece of cake. You should know that once you pick up this book, it will be next to impossible not to finish it. You are going to enjoy getting *Unstuck*! Thank you, Chris, for being so real and honest that each one of us can identify with our need to be unstuck."

—*Brian Simmons*
Stairway Ministries
Lead translator, The Passion Translation Project

UNSTUCK

HOPE FOR CHRISTIANS IN A DEAD-END JOB, DEAD-END FAITH, OR SOME SIMILAR SOUL-SHRIVELING RUT.

CHRIS DUPRÉ

WHITAKER
HOUSE

UNSTUCK:
Hope for Christians in a Dead-End Job, Dead-End Faith,
or Some Similar Soul-Shriveling Rut

ISBN: 978-1-62911-904-5 • eBook ISBN: 978-1-62911-905-2
Printed in the United States of America
© 2017 by Chris DuPré

Whitaker House
1030 Hunt Valley Circle
New Kensington, PA 15068
www.whitakerhouse.com

Library of Congress Cataloging-in-Publication Data

Names: DuPré, Chris, 1954– author.
Title: Unstuck / Chris DuPré.
Description: New Kensington, PA : Whitaker House, 2017. | Includes bibliographical references. |
Identifiers: LCCN 2017039473 (print) | LCCN 2017041593 (ebook) | ISBN 9781629119052 (e-book) | ISBN 9781629119045 (trade pbk. : alk. paper)
Subjects: LCSH: Midlife crisis—Religious aspects—Christianity.
Classification: LCC BV4579.5 (ebook) | LCC BV4579.5 .D87 2017 (print) | DDC 248.8/4—dc23
LC record available at https://lccn.loc.gov/2017039473

1 2 3 4 5 6 7 8 9 10 11 **ᴜᴊ** 24 23 22 21 20 19 18 17

TABLE OF CONTENTS

DEDICATION

Sometimes it's obvious who should receive a book dedication and other times it's more of a prayerful search. This one is like low-hanging fruit.

But it starts with a story.

In January of 2013, my wife and I took a trip to Kansas City. It seemed like a good time to visit a number of people whom we've known and loved for many years. We stayed with our lifelong friends, Russ and Kris Merwin. One evening while we were there, Russ and Kris took their youngest daughter, Laura, a freshman in high school at the time, to the doctor to see why she was feeling so poorly. Just a few hours later, Russ called me during dinner to tell me the life-changing news: Laura had just been diagnosed with leukemia. We wept and prayed, hoping and believing for the best.

The day after her diagnosis, Laura had surgery to install a porta-cath, a device used to give blood and also administer treatments. Laura's first twenty-eight-day round of chemo started the next day. This was a fast and difficult turnaround for an enthusiastic fourteen-year-old athlete who was full of life and energy. She was tested at the end of the round to confirm what her doctors were sure would arrest her type of leukemia. Unfortunately, due to the uniqueness of her disease, the chemo did not have the intended effect. In other words, it didn't work.

Over the next five months, Laura received three more rounds of chemo, each stronger than the previous one. There were countless side effects that Laura endured, including losing all her hair, total fatigue, nausea, sleepless nights, and sleepless days. She persevered and pressed through, choosing almost daily not to give in and give up. During one of Laura's chemo treatments, she had an anaphylactic shock reaction to a chemo drug. She would have died that day had it not been for the quick and lifesaving response of her nurses.

At the end of the fourth round of chemo, Laura's cancer was finally declared to be in remission. Due to the high probability that the leukemia could return, however, she needed the life-threatening and hopefully life-saving procedure of a bone marrow transplant. Life-threatening, because the pre-treatment for a bone marrow transplant requires the patient's entire immune system (bone marrow) to be killed through even stronger chemo drugs and multiple rounds of total body radiation. Laura was very weak and very sick for months afterwards.

Then, just before her transplant day, more hard news. Laura was diagnosed with a bad case of shingles, delaying her procedure for three more weeks. Finally, with a sister who was a perfect blood match, Laura went through the bone marrow transplant. After a period of time (which seemed to take forever) the results were in. The transplant was a success!

There was a five-month recovery from the bone marrow transplant procedure. In all, Laura spent seventy nights in the hospital; one stay lasted twenty-two days and another, thirty-two days. Not to mention the many daily trips she and her parents made back and forth from their house to the hospital.

Through all of 2013 and part of 2014 Laura was unable to attend high school because of weakness, fatigue, and a compromised immune system. Yet, Laura applied herself to her school work at home, studying with the help of visiting teachers and working diligently to stay on track. After over a year of being out of school Laura finally started attending her high school classes again. While beginning to slowly get her strength back, Laura injured her knee during a strengthening workout and had to have knee surgery. Laura eventually did finish up the last few months of her sophomore year with her classmates... on crutches.

In May 2016, Laura not only graduated from high school, but graduated with her class and with scholastic honors. With the help of scholarships from John Brown University, Laura is now a very successful sophomore at JBU where she is studying nursing. Her goal is to one day go back to the floor where she was treated as a patient, but this time as a pediatric oncology nurse.

I was there when the diagnosis came in and I watched her fight the cancer over the years. She changed her diet, declined a wig, received shots daily, got sick often, and endured many, many "bad news" events. In spite of all this, Laura was never a victim. *She never allowed herself to get "stuck" in depression or despair.* From the beginning, she was running for the prize of this all being over, so she could be who she felt called to be and do what she felt called to do.

Laura Merwin, thank you for displaying courage under fire. You are such an amazing example of what it means to be an overcomer, and I am humbled and honored to know you and call you a friend.

And so to you, Laura Merwin, one of my all-time heroes, I humbly dedicate this book.

FOREWORD

I just finished reading *Unstuck* by Chris DuPré. I was so caught up in the storytelling of this wonderful book that even before I finished it, I started to think of several people in my life who need to read it right now. No, really, I have a list of people I am buying it for and you will totally understand when you read it for yourself.

I have to commend this book and the writer to you for a minute. I have known Chris since the early nineties and to know Chris and his family is to know virtue. He has the gift of the wisdom you need even when you don't know what questions to ask.

Chris is a natural coach (as you can tell by all the sports references in this book), he has a church leadership background in both pastoring and worship leading (in other words, he knows how to herd cats), but really what makes this book special is that he is a father. Not just a dad to his girls, but a fatherly perspective toward each one of us who is stuck and needs a conversation to pull us out. Who would have that difficult conversation except a father who loves us?

As he walks you through various themes, such the hurdles of life, what hiddenness is for, and even how to navigate identity, it feels like you are getting poured into by someone who really knows and cares. Chris masterfully shares his wisdom but through deep empathy and concern for the reader. I love how Chris takes his own experiences and vulnerably shares them so we find ourselves inside of his process but also know the victory on the other side. Sometimes we are so focused on the solution, we forget that the painful process is usually part of the solution. From childhood stories all the way into his leadership experiences, Chris relates the realistic challenges we all face but gives us a chance to maybe see the process differently. His clear principles will recondition your thinking.

One of the greatest frustrations of the spiritual life is how easy it is to get stuck. And when you do get stuck, how do you get unstuck? How can Christians, who have the living God inside of them, overcome dry seasons of life where nothing they put effort toward seems to work out?

I know there have been times in my own life that I have felt stuck. What is hard is that many good-willed Christians tried to define the season *for* me and left me feeling like I had to work my way out of it instead of getting unstuck the way Chris defines it. It's amazing when you don't have mercy toward yourself how you can even become one of those good-willed, well-meaning Christians who give terrible advice. This book is different.

As you read this book, come out of performance. Don't use muscle and willpower to get out of the rut. Rather, rest in the principles that Chris gives and walk into the strong identity that he imparts. Let this beautiful book help you get *Unstuck*.

—*Shawn Bolz*
Author of *Translating God, God Secrets, Growing Up With God*
www.bolzministries.com

INTRODUCTION

It was school assembly day for my varsity soccer team. Our team was lined up in the middle of the gym floor, facing the rest of the school seated on the far side of the gym. I was dead center of the row of players. The coach went through the line, going from one end to the other and back again, talking about each player's strengths and thanking them for their play. Being in the center, I was the last one to be talked about—and the coach overlooked me. Enthusiastically, he turned to the school and said, "Let's give a big hand to this year's varsity team!" The team, as well as all the students shouted, "You forgot DuPré!" He turned around again and apologized. He then said a few kind and complimentary things, but the one thing that has stayed with me through the years is this: "Chris has the most potential of any athlete I've seen in a long line. The question is, will he fulfill that potential or will he always be known as Mr. Potential?" Everyone laughed and a few kids actually called me "Mr. Potential" for a while, but I was struck by his words. I told myself that I did not want to go through life being known as the guy who had so much potential but never quite fulfilled it.

I don't know anyone who would want that title! What keeps us from fulfilling our potential? As I look back on my life and observe the lives of those around me I am constantly amazed at how some people seem to grow wings and soar while others appear to stay in one spot, almost paralyzed, never venturing past their place of safety. Curious, I've asked many people why they never went after their dreams, and it resulted in some incredible conversations. The answer usually has something to do with fear, hurt, sin, laziness, rejection, pride, and wounding—they have attacked so many and put them in a holding pattern for years, if not their entire life. They're stuck! Completely stuck!

I grew up in a small town about thirty miles east of Rochester, NY. Winters there could be brutal. One year, I received some new boots for Christmas. I wore them proudly whenever and wherever I could, and when spring came, I found a new favorite pastime of finding puddles and stomping up and down in them. My super boots would protect me and keep me warm and dry. One day, I got off the bus and eyed a nice, new puddle. I took off and did my big jump, landing right in the middle. Unfortunately, this was not just any run-of-the-mill puddle. This one was made to capture people, and I was captured. I remember standing there feeling the cold water beginning to fill my boots…my new boots. I pulled one leg out, but no matter how much I pulled the other, it wouldn't move. My boot was stuck. I was stuck! A little frantic, I pulled and pulled until suddenly my leg came free. Unfortunately, my foot also came free of my boot. I pulled out my soaking wet sock and realized that one of my new boots was buried deep down in the slush.

My little mind was faced with a choice. Did I care enough about what's stuck to do something about it, or should I just leave my boot there and move on? I prized my boot so I had to think of a way for it to become unstuck. I found a stick and began to fish. After what seemed like an eternity, I finally pulled out my boot. That's the first time I ever went fishing and was actually glad that I got a boot instead of a fish.

My desire with this book is to address some of those "stuck" areas and hopefully provide a key that will open a door or two. I say a door or two, or even three, because it's almost always more than one thing. One muddy puddle seems to create another. Comparison creates pride, and pride creates jealousy, and so on. Ah, but God—He is the change factor in all of this and in Him we can find new life…life abundant!

A parable is told of a farmer who owned an old mule. The mule fell into the farmer's well. The farmer heard the mule "braying"—or whatever mules do when they fall into wells. After carefully assessing the situation, the farmer sympathized with the mule but decided that neither the mule nor the well was worth the trouble of saving. Instead, he called his neighbors together, told them what had happened, and then enlisted them to help haul dirt to bury the old mule in the well and put him out of his misery.

Initially, the old mule was hysterical! But as the farmer and his neighbors started shoveling and the first clump of dirt hit his back, a thought struck him. If every time a shovel-load of dirt landed on his back, he could shake it off and step up! This he did, blow after blow. "Shake it off and step up…shake it off and step up…shake it off and step up!" He repeated that line over and over again. No matter how painful the blows, or how distressing the situation seemed, the old mule fought panic and just kept right on shaking it off and stepping up!

It wasn't long before the old mule, battered and exhausted, stepped triumphantly over the wall of that well! What seemed like what had the potential to *bury* him, actually *blessed* him... all because of the manner in which he handled his adversity.

You and I were not made for mediocrity. We weren't made to sit on the ground and stare at the hurdle that just knocked us back. We weren't made to let life bury us alive. We were made to get up and we were made to overcome. First John 5:5 says, *"Who is he who overcomes the world, but he who believes that Jesus is the Son of God?"*

If you believe in Him, there is always a pathway to overcoming. As Paul says in Romans 8:31, 37, *"What then shall we say to these things? If God is for us, who can be against us?... Yet in all these things we are more than conquerors through Him who loved us."*

"Through Him who loved us...." That's the pathway to overcoming. My prayer is that as you go through the pages of this book, you will find Him, and in doing so, you will find your pathway to overcoming the hurdles that try to hinder you on this most incredible of journeys: life. May your journey be a blessed one!

SILENCING THE WHISPERS OF FEAR

Today, this comedian is a legend. But the first time he walked onstage, things didn't go as planned.

Maybe you know how it feels. You have a plan, you see yourself standing up there, your mind is perfectly clear, and you begin to do what you've been practicing at home for ages. Only this isn't home, and instead of telling your jokes to a supportive mirror, you're looking out over an audience that is looking back at you and waiting for you to either soar…or crash.

On this, his first night doing stand-up comedy, the young man got on stage and instantly did the one thing a comedian should never do…he froze. The crowd waited a few moments for him to get his rhythm but he never did. He stayed frozen.

The country club crowd soon began to jeer him and moments later he was booed off of the stage.

What would you do if this happened to you? Well, this young man refused to let that moment define him. He was not a hack and he knew it. He knew he was made to raise people's spirits but first he had to raise his own. He didn't let it fester, not even for a few days. Instead, he returned to the same club the next night, fought through his fears, stood up, and completed his set. The crowd roared with laughter and gave him a rowdy and heartfelt applause.

He did it! His name was Jerry Seinfeld, and the rest is history.

STAGE FRIGHT

I used to wonder what it would be like to be a stand-up comedian. Going from place to place, telling jokes, and making people laugh. That must be the world's greatest job...or so I thought. What could be better?

I remember watching a comedian on TV when I was a kid and laughing at his final joke. To this day I don't remember what it was but it made me laugh so loud that my mother and my brother, who were in the kitchen at the time, asked me what was so funny. I ran into the kitchen with visions of what I said making them howl and forever after remembering this moment in the kitchen as my first stand-up gig. I truly believed I was funny and that now was the time to show my family just how funny I could be.

I proudly stood in front of them. "There was this guy named...uh...there was this guy, his name was...."

I couldn't remember the guy's name. That was the basis of the whole joke and I couldn't remember his name. I completely froze!

My mother was so sweet. She just said, "Oh, that's alright Chris. You'll remember it at some point and when you do, come back in here and tell us." Unfortunately, she had to raise her voice over the sound of the laughter that was coming from the corner where my brother was sitting. I bombed and I knew it... and my brother knew it, too.

I immediately dropped my head, turned around, and with all the strength I could muster, I took that long walk of shame back to my place on the couch. Never again would I make that mistake!

Now, I don't blame my brother. If the roles were reversed I would have done the same thing. We were only fifteen months apart and we were on each other's case constantly. My mother used to call us the lion and the tiger. We were two alpha males from different "tribes" living in the same house.

What really plagued me was that I froze. I wondered if it would ever happen again. Wonder turned into overthinking, overthinking turned into a quiet anxiety, and my ongoing quiet anxiety turned into suppressed fear. This continued throughout high school. Whenever I was called upon to read out loud in class, if I messed up a word or read something incorrectly, the anxiety would descend, these feelings would begin to boil up inside my gut, and then, *WHAM*, the words in front of me would begin to become blurry and finally a black cloud would overtake my vision. I couldn't even see the words. I was more than just frozen at that point—I was paralyzed!

This internal battle against fear set in motion an obsessive desire to manipulate my circumstances so that what I feared would never cross my path.

All through high school, if I knew that the upcoming class would involve reading aloud, I would either tell the teacher that I was suffering with a bad headache or that I needed reading glasses and it was difficult for me to read for very long. With those excuses, I almost always got out of reading. I also made a point of avoiding any kind of oral report. If reading would make me shudder, what would speaking in front of people make me do? I didn't even want to imagine it.

College, unfortunately, was more of the same. At age nineteen I became a believer and began to write songs. People would hear about them or hear me sing from another room and ask me to play for them. I wanted so much to sing for people, but fear would raise its ugly head and I'd be paralyzed all over again. The only way that I would let anyone hear my songs was if they stayed in one room while I played from another. I needed to not see them and I needed them to not see me. Often I would go into the bathroom and have them stay in the living room. (The perk was that our bathroom had tiled walls and it always sounded amazing when I sang and played in there.)

These stories may either sound horribly familiar or like I'm making a big deal out of nothing. To those who have never had to deal with a crippling fear, people with one may appear weak—mentally, physically, and spiritually. "Come on, Chris," they might say, "God hasn't given us a spirit of fear, but of power, love, and a sound mind." But fear is powerful and can be an ongoing struggle, even for the most fervent believers. What fear did to me was shut down my eyes, my voice, and my mind, turning my thoughts and my gifts into nothing more than prisoners. That's the purpose of fear. Its desire is to keep you from effectively moving in your unique gifts and callings.

NOT GIVEN A SPIRIT OF FEAR

Let's look at that Scripture about fear that I referenced above. It's from 2 Timothy 1:7 and reads, *"For God has not given us a spirit of fear, but of power and of love and of a sound mind."*

This is a wonderful truth from the Word of God and it has encouraged and empowered multitudes throughout every generation. Its purpose, though, is more than just a "hearty word of needed power" for the moment. We need to sometimes take a closer look at Scripture and see its initial intent.

As an example, take one of the most well-known and beloved Scriptures: *"For God so loved the world that He gave His only begotten Son, that whosoever believes in Him should not perish but have everlasting life"* (John 3:16). If we look at it closer, we will see something amazing. The simple word *"so"* lends us great insight. Today, the word *so* is often used to refer to quantity, causing us to read the verse like this: "He loves us *'so'* much that He gave His only begotten Son." The meaning of *so* at the time of the writing of the King James Version actually had a different meaning. It meant "in this way." If we use it that way the passage becomes more beautiful and unique. "For God loved the world in this way, that He gave...." It's beautiful both ways but this version directs our heart to see God's intent.

So it is with Paul's second letter to Timothy. He states that God didn't give us a spirit of fear but of power, love, and a sound mind. If we take this by itself, it is encouraging and helpful information, giving us added empowerment to take on life. But if we see it in its larger context, we can then see God's desire for us to flourish in our lives and in our ministry. Turn the page back to the fourth chapter of 1 Timothy where Paul is encouraging Timothy to press into his calling to be a leader in spite of his youth and experience. Paul saw who Timothy really was and wanted to encourage him in spite of his young age or his lack of experience. That's what good leaders do.

Paul then told him that others believed in him and supported that belief by standing with him. He tells Timothy, *"Do not neglect your gift, which was given you through prophecy when the body of elders laid their hands on you"* (1 Timothy 4:14 NIV). Paul is telling Timothy that not only is he a gifted young man, other more mature believers believed in him so much that they laid hands on him and prayed for him to boldly do what God had gifted him to do.

This is where the rubber meets the road. We are all gifted in one way or another. It's what we do with those gifts that determines everything. Timothy obviously needed a little push from Paul, who knew him and knew what was in him.

WE ARE ALL GIFTED IN ONE WAY OR ANOTHER. IT'S WHAT WE DO WITH THOSE GIFTS THAT DETERMINES EVERYTHING.

It doesn't stop here, though. Now, I may be reading into this, but it seems that in spite of what Paul wrote to Timothy, Timothy didn't completely walk out Paul's admonition in 1 Timothy. Somehow Paul must have gotten reports that though Timothy was an excellent young man, he was still holding back from exercising his gifts. Why else would Paul repeat himself, almost word for word, in 2 Timothy 1:6? He says, *"Therefore I remind you to stir up the gift of God which is in you through the laying on of my hands."* The difference here is that Paul doesn't just say that he remembers the moment when the elders prayed for Timothy. He remembered something more personal. Paul now says that it was *"through the laying on of my hands."* Paul was more than a witness, he was a participant. He laid hands on Timothy because he saw greatness in the young man.

In the same way, there is greatness in you. You were not created to be a spectator throughout your life. Your gifts were given to you for a purpose. They were never intended to be hidden and occasionally enjoyed for yourself. You have gifts so that you can be a gift.

And fear steals those gifts.

FEAR: THE WORLD'S SNEAKIEST THIEF

In the very next verse I believe that we see the cause of Timothy's hesitation: *"For God has not given us a spirit of fear, but of power and of love and of a sound mind"* (2 Timothy 1:7). We all know this Scripture, but for most people it's our go-to verse for moments when we become frightened about something external, such as fearing bad news or being afraid of the dark. Those are great times to remember that we were not given a spirit of fear, but what Paul is trying to address is something specific that he sees in Timothy—Timothy neglecting to use his gifts. This verse is about fear in the context of releasing our gifts. That's why it's located here and not elsewhere.

Timothy was afraid of something. Of what we do not know, but Paul realized that it was affecting him in the areas of power, love, and soundness of mind.

Fear does that. Whatever fear was gripping Timothy, it was stealing from him his very life and calling. Paul wasn't addressing the peripheral fears that we may all carry, though each fear we carry is an added weight that God wants to release from us. Paul was attempting to zero in on specific fears that hinder, and often halt, the unique ministry that we each carry.

My specific fear growing up was speaking or singing in front of people. That fear totally shut me down. Like I said, I would always try to remove myself from any situation in which I would have to read, talk, or sing in front of people. I even left the room more than once to get physically sick. It's true. One time I was playing in a band and they gave me a one-sentence solo line in the middle of the song, known as the bridge. Up until this time I would play guitar and sing backup but I never would sing anything by myself. During practice, I got through the bridge because there was only a handful of us, but when we went live with a full house, everything changed. The band's leader looked at me and thought I was okay, but as the song progressed I became gripped with fear. He could see I was melting down, and in spite of the horror on his face, I set my guitar down, walked offstage, ran outside, and vomited. I then went around to the front of the building, walked in, and watched the band finish the song. I waved at them but they didn't seem too happy.

I knew that my heart's desire was to sing and speak before others but when I tried, I was shut down. Unfortunately, fear knows no bounds. It attacks us at every turn, whispering its demonic voice into our soul, trying to steer us down a path of frustration, inaction, and eventually total detachment. At least, it looks like detachment, but to us, inside, it feels like a prison.

When I did some research on the different types of fears, I found one list that came to sixty-eight, and believe it or not, that's just for the ones that started with the letter "A"! I'm absolutely serious! I'm not sure of the final tally. But, just for those who are interested, here are a few of the fears that I had no idea actually existed:

Politicophobia: Fear or abnormal dislike of politicians

Omphalophobia: Fear of belly buttons

Aulophobia: Fear of flutes

Chorophobia: Fear of dancing

Kathisophobia: Fear of sitting down

Novercaphobia: Fear of your stepmother

(I had a great stepmother but there's a chance that I had to deal with the fear of dancing when I was in junior high school.)

As I perused the whole list I was struck with one thing: fear is waiting for us around every corner. I realize that some of these fears may sound ridiculous, but to those who suffer, it's anything but funny.

Where does fear raise its ugly head in your life? Is it the fear of failure, or an unknown of the future that keeps you up at night? Do you fear not having a fulfilling life? For many, this is a result of comparison. We compare our lives with those around us and for some reason we always come up short. Bring in social media and suddenly we are seeing over and over again images of the perfect couple, the perfect family, and the perfect life. After a while, all we can see is what we don't have instead of seeing all the blessings that we actually do have.

REGAINING POWER

So, how do we walk out of all these fears? How can we regain power, love, and a sound mind in order to live in our giftings?

When fear attacks, power is trapped within us. We have two options when we're confronted by something fearful: fight or flight. If we overcome fear, we become fighters, standing against the foe before us. But when fear begins to have its way, flight takes over. It can make us run, or it can make us freeze. It can turn our arms and legs to rubber. Or cause a dark cloud to come down and envelop your sight. Or make your insides feel like they want to become your outsides. Or all of the above. It's not pretty.

I love this quote from Richie Norton: "To escape fear, you have to go through it, not around." There is no other way. We have to go *through* fear. I'm not saying going through fear is easy. Fear is tormenting—that's what the apostle John says in 1 John 4. Look at verse 18. It reads: *"There is no fear in love; but perfect love casts out fear, because fear involves torment. But he who fears has not been made perfect in love."* John is not condemning anyone because they are battling fears. He is inviting them into a deeper understanding of the love of God in order to overcome them. The revelation of God's affection is where the power flows into and from our being. Love is not just a white fluffy cloud of pleasant thoughts. It's best exemplified by one Man being beaten, whipped, and nailed to a cross. That's definitely not a cute, pretty, uplifting picture. But it's a power that saves, heals, and delivers.

If we try to fight on our own, the fight will always eventually turn to flight. If we just see ourselves and our own power confronting fear we will allow our thoughts of past failures to determine of future endeavors. We can't let that happen. Fear is real, but when confronted with the power of God's love it has to bow. Fear wants to present itself larger and more powerful than God's capacity to overcome it, but in reality, it's not a fair fight. It's never two equals battling each other. God is God, and when we hide ourselves in Him, He can and will overcome anything.

REGAINING LOVE

As I said before, when I was first saved I was playing guitar and writing songs but I wasn't letting anyone hear them. Oh, I'd let people hear my songs but it was always in a small group. And by *small* I mean *very small*…as in, one or two people. Then I wrote a song that everyone (or at least those I let listen to it) actually felt was great. My brother Mark asked me to sing it at our Sunday night service. Of course I said no. He then said that he would sing it if I played behind him. I agreed to that.

When it came time to play I got on stage and, much to my horror, found that there was a vocal mic for me. Mark said it was there in case I wanted to sing backup but that he was still planning on singing the song. He did ask me to sing along if I felt comfortable. My brother started out by standing in front of me, a little to my left. I felt very comfortable with him blocking my view, or, should I say, *others'* view of *me*.

As the song began, I may have sung along a bit but I was barely audible. As the song progressed, I began to get lost in its melody and words. I heard my brother singing and I tried some harmonies, but after a short while, I really didn't notice who was singing what. As the song began to wind down to its final verse, I realized that my brother was hardly singing. But I could hear him—or could I? No, it was *my* voice that was singing. I was there, singing in front of a group of people, and I wasn't getting sick. As a matter of fact, I was feeling empowered. I was feeling great. I was doing what burned in my heart to do.

By the end of the song I realized that another shift had taken place. My brother was no longer in front of me. He was now behind me to my left. My brother had placed love between me and my fear, knocking it out of my life. He believed in me and found a creative way for me to not "go around" my fear but to "go through it." He became a hero to me that day, and as I look back on over forty years of ministering to people in song, leading worship, speaking, teaching, or just sharing my heart, I have never forgotten what he did for me that Sunday night in 1974. Until that night, I was void of power, but *my brother's love attacked my fear and brought me liberty.* As John says in 1 John 4:18, "*...fear involves torment, but he who fears has not been made perfect in love.*"

Steven Pressfield writes in his best seller, *The War of Art,*

> Like self-doubt, fear is an indicator. Fear tells us what we have to do. The more scared we are of a work or calling, the more sure we can be that we have to do it. Resistance is experienced as fear; the degree of fear equates to the strength of Resistance.[1]

---

1. Steven Pressfield, *The War of Art* (New York: Black Irish Books, 2002), 40.

Paul saw the gifting in Timothy and he also saw the resistance. When fear and love meet, something bizarre happens. Though someone may truly care about another, even love them, fear distorts that love and produces a horrible obsession called jealousy. Many may love those around them, but if they fear that they will be overshadowed or even left behind because of the gifting of others, a spirit of jealousy begins to creep in and distort what once was a pure love.

Look at married couples where love exists but where fear has found a foothold. If there's a suspicion of unfaithfulness, even if there is no history or not even a hint of that kind of activity, either in action or in word, it can still be agony. If someone carries the burden of having a jealous spouse, they are greatly hindered from becoming the man or woman they're meant to be because so much time and energy is wasted on overcompensating for their spouse's fears. The same is true for those who work with or minister with others who cast a dark shadow of fear or jealousy. Creative juices and spontaneity are stymied when you work with a fearful or jealous person.

In contrast, let me tell you about the time I was watching *Beauty and the Beast* with my wife, Laura, and our granddaughter. At the end, right after the Beast's transformation, my granddaughter asked, "How did the Beast change back into a prince?" I hesitated for a moment trying to come up with something pithy when my wife calmly replied, "She just loved his ugly parts away." I was stunned. Not that my wife would or could say something like that—she's brilliant—but by the truth of those words. They penetrated my heart. To this day, that is how I know we can remove our "ugly parts."

REGAINING A SOUND MIND

And let's not forget soundness of mind. Paul also addresses this area of attack from fear. How many of us have been in situation where we feel comfortable, where we're "in our groove," only to have a fear abruptly drop in and ruin our peace of mind? One minute we are thinking perfectly clearly and the next minute we find ourselves in a fearful and intimidating situation and our brain is no longer working the way it should. Lucid thoughts turn into chaotic thoughts, or worse, into no thoughts at all.

What did that? A spirit of fear. It attacks your soundness of mind. That's why I couldn't stand in front of others and talk. Not only did I feel as if I was about to blackout, I felt as if brain cells were actually jumping out of my ears, leaving me with no ability to remember or process what was happening.

WE FEAR EXPOSING OUR FEAR, AND YET, THE GREATEST CHANCE OF VICTORY IS FOUND WHEN IT'S FINALLY BROUGHT INTO THE LIGHT.

But then you go home. You lay down for the night and begin to play back the day. Suddenly everything becomes clear. You know exactly what you should have done and exactly what you should have said. You can't wait until you have another chance to redeem yourself. But when the chance comes again, and you're looking inside your mind for the right words, the spirit of intimidation once again washes them right out. It's as if someone took a power sprayer and focused it on the thoughts you had just whitewashed on the side of your brain. Or like a house that is caught in a rainstorm right in the middle of a paint job.

Fear wants to control you. It wants to own you. If the enemy of your soul can't keep you from the new life found within the kingdom of God, he will send fear to keep the kingdom of God locked within you. Fear will place an invisible fence around you. You may hate your fear or even obsess about it, but you will do everything in your power so that no one else will see your fear. We fear exposing our fear, and yet, the greatest chance of victory is found when it's finally brought into the light.

I was a very good athlete and a leader in my school. The last thing I wanted to do was to come across as weak or fearful, so I told no one of my fears and went on about my business, manipulating things here and there in order to not allow myself to be put into a scenario that would expose any of my fears. This continued until the desire to fulfill my call became more important than the desire to hide my fear. It was then that I found love, love that brought deliverance and brought me a completely new life.

At some point, something needs to become more important than the fear we're carrying. Until then, fear is king. We need to see another goal as being more important to our lives than always giving in to fear.

I love the prophetic word given to Zacharias in Luke chapter 1. He is describing God's eternal desire, which has been from the beginning, to save and to deliver His people. He points to the promise given to Abraham and says,

> *That we should be saved from our enemies, and from the*
> *hand of all who hate us,*
> *To perform the mercy promised to our fathers*
> *And to remember His holy covenant,*
> *The oath which He swore to our father Abraham:*
> *To grant us that we,*
> *Being delivered from the hand of our enemies,*
> *Might **serve Him without fear**....*"   (Luke 1:71–74)

That we might *"serve Him without fear."* That's a beautiful thing. A life without fear. Our goal, His desire.

WINNING THE BATTLE

Let me share with you one last story. I was helping to oversee the worship community as a wonderful group of comrades began what is now known as the International House of Prayer in Kansas City. I had been the worship pastor with Mike Bickle at a nearby church and I moved over, not as the worship pastor, but as the senior worship leader. It was more of a fatherly role as opposed to any other type of organizational leadership role. I led the main sessions and was the main worship leader for all of our conferences. I was also "Dad."

By this time we were running 24/7, and every time slot was filled in with worship teams and prayer leaders. I began to hear about a young woman who was singing in the "Night Watch," the time between midnight and 6:00 a.m. Apparently, she was a bit fearful about singing in front of large groups but I was encouraged to come and listen. One evening, late at night, I snuck into the back of IHOP and listened to her sing. It was wonderful. She had a simplicity and beauty that was undeniable.

I loved the ministry of those whose labor of love sustained the flow of worship and prayer during the night season, but I asked myself, was she here for that reason or was she here for another reason? Was she possibly singing at night out of nervousness or fear of the larger crowds that went with the day sessions? It was time for me to find out.

I initially asked her how she felt about coming onto my team and being a part of the day meetings and conferences. She thanked me but instantly rejected the offer. I tried a couple of more times but between her love of the Night Watch and her hesitation of being a part of my larger sessions, she continued to say no.

One day I asked her if she would have coffee with me as I had some thoughts I wanted to bounce off of her. She agreed and we met at a local coffee shop connected to our ministry. What she didn't know was that I had already met with Mike and told him that although I felt she would be wonderful on my team, she would not leave the Night Watch. I asked him if he would help me out with this. He said he would and asked me what I had in mind.

Now kids, what I'm about to share could be considered dangerous, so please, don't do this at home! I asked Mike to come into the coffee shop where we were meeting and to personally ask her about coming on my team. My "plan" was to have him walk by our table, start up a conversation, tell her that she would be a real asset to my team, and then, as if it was a momentary God thought, ask her to seriously consider coming on my team. He did, but instantly she said she had already told me no. Without skipping a beat, he asked her again if she would prayerfully consider doing it. I don't know if it was the look on his face or the tone of his voice, but ten seconds later she did an about-turn, and before I knew it, she was on my team.

The only thing was, she still seemed tentative. She held back from singing and didn't sing out prophetically at all. She was a different person from the one I had heard in the Night Watch. After a couple of weeks I decided to take matters into my own hands. (Again, don't do this at home.) During a set, I turned to the crowd and said, "Now, we're going to have a prophetic song sung over those gathered here." I then turned away from her and waited. For thirty long seconds the music continued without any singing. Finally she began...and it was beautiful.

After the worship set she came up to me, pointed her finger at me and said, "Please don't ever do that to me again!" I looked her in the eye and said, "How did it feel when you were done?" She didn't change the serious expression on her face but quietly said, "Great." I did the same thing again a week or so later when she continued to hold back, and when we finished she looked at me and said, "I get it. I've been battling anxiety concerning singing in front of larger groups but I get it. I'll sing out." That was the last time she held back. From that moment on she was stellar!

Oh, yeah, her name was Misty Edwards, and to this day she continues to be stellar!

If we're honest and look at the areas in our lives where fear has an inroad we can begin the journey out of fear and into liberty. Truth brings freedom and a free believer is a very dangerous thing. *Good* dangerous!

2

IT'S OKAY TO REJECT REJECTION

What would you do if you were fired from your job because, as your boss said, you lacked imagination and had no good ideas? That's exactly what happened to this man. He was living in Kansas City at the time and was working for the local city newspaper, *The Kansas City Star*. If we're honest with ourselves, many of us would become either discouraged, depressed, or decidedly angry.

This man became great instead.

He started one business after another. Unfortunately, each business ended in failure and he eventually went bankrupt. After all that, most of us would say, "Okay, time to put a fork in it," or in other words, find a quiet place to slink away, look for a safe job, and live with our unfulfilled dreams drying up inside our hearts.

This man, though, wouldn't quit. He started a business that began to do well and, over time, he built himself a very successful career. Still, he wasn't satisfied. He was sure there were more things he was called to do. He took his proven accomplishments to a bank to ask for financing for his dream. But one financial institution after another turned him down. Rejection is a terrible thing, but only if we let it become a terrible thing. This guy refused. For him, rejection was only an incentive to buckle down and present his ideas with more wisdom and vision.

All in all, three hundred and two potential financial backers, both institutions and individuals, turned him down. Still, he was determined to see his vision come to pass. And, finally, financial backer number three hundred and three said *yes*. After years of waiting and longing he began to build his dream, a dream that we know today as Disneyland.

The man, of course, was Walt Disney.

By the way, years later Walt Disney returned to Kansas City and purchased *The Kansas City Star*. Who would have ever imagined?

What kind of person continues to press on when surrounded by so much resistance? The kind of person who can be like an airplane. Planes don't take off *with* the wind, they take off going straight *into* the wind, for it's the wind that gives it lift. The same with an eagle or a hawk. When they want to soar, they don't fly with the wind, they fly straight into it.

What Walt Disney dealt with in his early days was basic rejection, and he flew straight into it. I say "basic" rejection because rejection in its basic form happens to us all and has no real power on its own. How we see and handle rejection is what gives it power—either the power to give us lift or the power to tear us down. Disney chose to let it lift him.

REJECTION IS INEVITABLE

Over the years, I have had the great privilege of meeting and getting to know successful people from many different types of businesses, callings, and arenas of life. But no matter how successful they've become, none of them have been able to avoid rejection.

Let's take famous King David as an example. Before he became king, the biblical David was young, handsome, and filled with wisdom. He was loved by those in authority and admired by both men and women. Everything seemed to be going his way. I guess that's what happens when you kill the greatest threat to your land, a braggadocio giant name Goliath. The current king, Saul, showed the brave young David incredible favor:

> *Now when he had finished speaking to Saul, the soul of Jonathan was knit to the soul of David, and Jonathan loved him as his own soul. Saul took him that day, and would not let him go home to his father's house anymore. Then Jonathan and David made a covenant, because he loved him as his own soul. And Jonathan took off the robe that was on him and gave it to David, with his armor, even to his sword and his bow and his belt. So David went out wherever Saul sent him, and behaved wisely. And Saul set him over the men of war, and he was accepted in the sight of all the people and also in the sight of Saul's servants.*
>
> (1 Samuel 18:1–5)

Amazing. Here he was, this little shepherd boy, the youngest son who often received the least amount of honor, now ushered into a new world where every honor known to the kingdom is coming his way. He has access to the king and the king's son becomes his closest friend—so close, in fact, that their relationship is spoken of and extolled even to this day. Everywhere he went he acted with wisdom, which opened even more doors. Eventually, King Saul set him over all of his men of war. In a culture like that, where war was common, this was the greatest honor a man could have. Then, suddenly, it all came tumbling down.

> *Now it had happened as they were coming home, when David was returning from the slaughter of the Philistine, that the women had come out of all the cities of Israel, singing and dancing, to meet King Saul, with tambourines, with joy, and with musical instruments.*　　　　(verse 6)

I can just see King Saul sauntering down the road. "Another day, another battle, and another victory. My journey home should be sweet. Oh, yeah, here come the ladies. I just love this part. Okay, ladies, here I am, sing it out!"

> *So the women sang as they danced, and said: "Saul has slain his thousands, and David his ten thousands."*
> 　　　　　　　　　　　　　　　　　　　　　(verse 7)

"What! What are they singing? What did they just say about David? He kills ten thousand for every thousand I kill? NO!!!"

Suddenly things began to change. Check out Saul's response:

> *Then Saul was very angry, and the saying displeased him; and he said, "They have ascribed to David ten thousands, and to me they have ascribed only thousands. Now what more can he have but the kingdom?" So Saul eyed David from that day forward.*　　　　(verses 8–9)

In the blink of eye—or, more accurately, with just a few lyrics from some ladies— everything changed for David. His relationship with Saul was never the same. Saul saw the favor of God all over David and his jealousy rose up to the point where he tried a number of times to kill him.

Having a former friend, especially if he's a king, try to get you killed is right up there with the worst forms of rejection a man can endure. One minute David is the larger-than-life hero of the land and the next minute he is on the run from the king, the father of his best friend. And yet, it's in this atmosphere that David shines the most. Though Saul had just thrown a spear to try to kill him, David remained loyal to Saul, never trying to either fight back or usurp Saul's authority. Instead, he pressed into God for wisdom in order to not react to Saul, but to instead act with God's heart. Listen to how the chapter comes to a close.

> *Thus Saul saw and knew that the LORD was with David, and that Michal, Saul's daughter, loved him; and Saul was still more afraid of David. So Saul became David's enemy continually. Then the princes of the Philistines went out to war. And so it was, whenever they went out, that David behaved more wisely than all the servants of Saul, so that his name became highly esteemed.*   (verses 28–30)

"*David behaved more wisely….*" What great words! Especially considering all that's happening to him. One minute he's the "man" and then next he's the "wanted man." This must have hurt David very much. He had been beloved by Saul, but now he was a fugitive. Remember, too, that before David even came into Saul's court, he had been anointed by the prophet Samuel to be the next king. Hidden inside his heart was that assurance—or would a better word be *anguish?* I can imagine him crying out in prayer, *Lord, I thought I was supposed to be Your anointed! So why am I being hunted by my former friend the king?*

We often carry words and dreams and lifelong desires inside of our hearts, only to have everything suddenly go downhill. If it's because of an accidental situation such as the downsizing of a company or some other circumstance outside of our control, we soon see the bigger picture and realize that God is the one who really is in control. But when our dreams, hopes, and desires are dashed because of the sin or weakness of another human being, like Saul almost dashed David's, it becomes much more difficult to bounce back.

We fuse that person in our mind and in our heart to the negative situation until at last we find ourselves carrying them and the pain together as one. For some reason it seems to blind us to God's heart and His presence in whatever circumstances we find ourselves in at the moment. The person that brought our hurt and rejection is now, in our minds, bigger than God.

But it is much too difficult to press through the rejection you're experiencing when you're carrying an unforgiven person on your back. Do yourself a favor and let them off at the next bus stop. When you do, the load will become so much lighter and you will become so much freer to get back to what you were made to do.

REJECTION CAN BE A SPRINGBOARD

To some, rejection is the end of a dream. To others, it's just the beginning.

For me, it was…well, let me tell you about it.

Shortly after I was saved I joined a music group and also became one of the worship leaders in our church. It helped that I played guitar and that people didn't scream or run out of the building when I sang. I did that for many years and have always enjoyed leading worship. But after about twelve years, I began to feel a call to preach. I had never had any formal training, but I hoped that one day I could learn the art of public speaking.

One Sunday, as the church service was coming to a close, the pastor announced that he was going to lead a class on teaching and preaching. I was so excited. *Here's my chance*, I thought. He then said that it was a closed class and that he had already picked those from the congregation whom he felt should be in the class. I was sure I'd been picked. He closed the service and mentioned that there was a sheet in the back of the church with the names he'd chosen for the class. He concluded, "If you don't see your name on the list and you feel strongly about being in the class, come see me and I'll pray about whether you should join the group."

After the last, "Amen," I joined the throng that went to the back and began to search for their names. After looking it over (more than once) I finally let it sink in…*I'm not on the list, I'm not in the class*. I went back to the platform and gathered up my guitar, my Bible, and my coat. As I made my way toward the exit I saw the pastor standing alone. I wasn't going to let a piece of paper keep me from a desire of my heart. I called out to him to wait, set my things down, and walked over to him. I told him that I would really love to be in that class. I let him know that teaching and preaching was something that I felt God had in store for me in the days ahead.

(Now, this pastor was, and still is, a good man and a long-time friend. I love him and appreciate all he did for me over the years and if he reads this I know he will find the humor in it.) After I shared my heart, he put his arm around me and patted my shoulder. A shoulder pat is never a good sign. Neither were his first words. He said, "Chris, Chris…." When someone starts out a sentence by using your name twice, you know it's not going to end well. It's like when your mother calls you by your first and middle name.

He continued, "You're just a worship leader. Musicians don't normally become speakers and speakers don't usually venture into music. I think you need to ask God to help you be satisfied with who you are and what you're doing." I knew I wasn't supposed to argue so I thanked him for his time and headed home. I told my wife later about the incident and she immediately said, "Did he pray about it? He said that if someone asked him to be in the class, he would pray about it." I told her that no, I'm sure he didn't. So, knowing he took Mondays off, I made an appointment to see him first thing Tuesday morning.

I was ushered into his office shortly after 9:00 a.m. on Tuesday and sat down. When I told him that he had never prayed about my request he nodded and then bowed his head. *He's praying right here, right now? He's not going to go home and really pray about it?* I was starting to feel a little sheepish about the whole thing. But after about thirty seconds or so he lifted his head, grabbed a piece of paper, and wrote down, "The truth will set you free." He handed me the paper and said, "You're on for a week from Sunday for the 9:00 a.m. Bible Study and that's your message." I asked him if I could do something that was on my heart and he said, "No, that's your message. If you're called to teach we'll know it when you're done. If you're not called to teach, well, we'll know that too."

I sat in silence for a moment and then realized that God had given me an amazing opportunity. I smiled, stood up, and shook his hand while thanking him for the opportunity. I then walked out and began to wonder whether I'd done the right thing in coming here. I mean, I could ruin everything if I bombed. I've never spoken in public except for one-liners as I've lead worship, but now I had to fill up forty-five minutes of time with people watching, some wondering why I was up there and not them.

I then prayed that most universal prayer, "Oh God, help me!"

And help me He did. The next day the paper arrived and on the front page was a picture of a man walking out of prison with his hands extended high into the air and in big bold letters above that picture was the headline "The Truth Will Set You Free!" It was an article about how DNA testing was helping to solve crimes and, in so doing, innocent people were being set free. I had the perfect springboard to begin, and as I did, the rest just flowed easily. I felt God's hand on it and was confident that He would be there.

A week and a half later I stood before the church with the pastor in the front row and square in my line of vision, and I began to share my heart. I wasn't polished, but I was real, and I felt prepared. I shared not only what was in my notes, but out of the blue I was also receiving downloads of revelation as the teaching went on. I felt His presence every step of the way. When I finished, something happened that I had never before seen in our Sunday morning Bible studies. I received a standing ovation from my church family. I must admit, my eyes became a little moist as I stood there and took it all in.

Then suddenly I saw the pastor stand up and head my way. He was the first person to reach me. He put his hands on my shoulders and leaned in to speak something quietly for my ears alone. "That was wonderful. Now, don't take my class. It will ruin what you have. I'll be putting you on the rotation to speak." With that he turned around and walked away. He was good to his word. From that moment on I was not just on the rotation, but I was granted a new life in God. I was now given the gift of stewarding His Word and His life, both in me and through me. I am forever grateful for this man's bravery to let me speak, as well as his humility when I finished. I am also grateful to God for helping me push through the initial rejection. Sometimes the next push opens the next door.

STUCK IN REJECTION

Some doors, though, just don't open up. And if we're honest with ourselves, we know we need to evaluate whether *we* are the problem. Is it possible that the precious gift that God has placed within us is being held captive because of the way we carry ourselves and interact with others?

A man approached me years ago while I was overseeing the worship at a church in Kansas City. "I'd like to play bass on your team," he informed me. "Your bass player is okay, but I could blow him out of the water."

I held my tongue and invited him to join us at our next practice. I wanted to see if he was as arrogant as he first appeared or if his introduction was a case of nerves or poor people skills. When he came to our Saturday practice I asked him to sit and watch for a while. I told him that community was a very important element with our team and that I'd like him to get to know some folks. After a bit, the pizza arrived. (You gotta have pizza on Saturday worship practice.) He grabbed a piece and walked away from everyone. He sat alone, even though he was invited to join the group. A couple of people even went over to him but quickly sensed that he wanted nothing to do with them. He was just waiting for me to let him play.

After practice he came up to me with a fire in his eyes. "Aren't you going to have me play?" he asked curtly. I told him I was more interested in having him meet and know the team and that I would eventually have him play, probably at our next practice. He grabbed his bass and said, "You blew it! You could have had me playing bass for you but I'm leaving. You just lost the best bass player you're ever had."

Honestly, I didn't blow it nor did I lose anything. Would he have been an asset? I'm sure his bass playing was amazing and that he would have added a level of musicianship that we needed. Unfortunately, his character made it impossible for me to invite him into our group. His pain, hurt, pride, and arrogance brought about his rejection from our team.

Now, I'm not calling on everyone to begin a life of constant internal inspection. That wouldn't be good. But, if you find yourself going around the mountain again and again, you may need to ask yourself some honest questions.

+ Am I doing something that results in the same outcome over and over again?

+ Am I aware of how my actions affect the people around me?

+ Am I so focused on my situation (whatever that is) that I miss the journey of others?

It's good to be honest with yourself, but better yet, find a friend that loves you deeply and has your best interest in mind. Ask someone who loves you the hard questions you may be afraid to ask yourself. As it says in Proverbs 27:6, *"Faithful are the wounds of a friend."*

WHEN WE EXPERIENCE REJECTION IN ONE FORM OR ANOTHER WE UNKNOWINGLY SET INTO MOTION NOT JUST THE OUTCOME OF OUR PRESENT CIRCUMSTANCES, BUT A POTENTIALLY SCRIPTED RESPONSE FOR FUTURE SITUATIONS.

Some things may be hard to hear, but if we can hear truth, our lives might just take the turn that we've been praying about for many years.

If we don't ask ourselves the tough questions, we risk rejection becoming a self-fulfilling prophecy. When we experience rejection in one form or another we unknowingly set into motion not just the outcome of our present circumstances, but a potentially scripted response for future situations. It's never a question of "if" we'll have to face rejection again. There will always be a next time. But how we have dealt with it in the past will help set a course for dealing with it in the future…or not dealing with it.

If you expect rejection, you will see it around every corner. As a matter of fact, you will see it where it doesn't even exist. I can often feel a spirit of rejection coming from a person after only a few moments in their presence. They seem to be pulling away from me, not expecting that I will engage them, or that, if I do, I will suddenly pull the rug out from under them. They apologize constantly and are usually the first to end the conversation so that they will be the one in control of the parting, thus avoiding being rejected by me.

It's such a sad way to live because they never feel free to be themselves. Because of this, they rarely find themselves in a place where they can freely express the wonderful gifts that God has put within them. Their circle is very small, they say things like, "Only a couple of people really understand me," and they don't see that the cloud of rejection that swirls around them has an effect on every single relationship that they encounter.

If we're all honest we would probably say that at some point, or with certain people, we have been in the same situation. We expected pushback, disapproval, or even the cold shoulder, and we got it. At that point, we become programmed to "expect it and receive it." We push off the problem on the other person even though those around you have never experienced what you have with them.

REJECTION OF CHRIST

The better way to deal with rejection is to remember that it came to Christ, and He said it would come to us, too—not because of who *we* are, but because of who *He* is. The one rejection where we can actually find joy is the rejection given to us for the sake of the gospel. Jesus said in Luke 6:22–23, *"Blessed are you when men hate you, and when they exclude you, and revile you, and cast out your name as evil, for the Son of Man's sake. Rejoice in that day and leap for joy! For indeed your reward is great in heaven…."*

Now, I don't like being rejected for any reason, but when my life mirrors God's heart in such a way that someone takes notice and attempts to attack Him through me, well, that's one rejection I can feel good about. (I was going to say that it's one rejection I can live with, but in today's world, you never know.) The vast majority of rejection that comes our way has nothing to do with us. David did not do anything wrong to have Saul become jealous and murderous in his heart. That was Saul's weakness, not David's.

Take a look at Isaiah 53:3: *"He was despised and rejected by men, a Man of sorrows and acquainted with grief. And we hid, as it were, our faces from Him; He was despised, and we did not esteem Him."* Obviously, Jesus did nothing wrong to bring upon Himself the rejection of the men who would capture, torture, and eventually kill Him. On the contrary, He walked in meekness and humility and was the perfect example of love upon the earth. In spite of that, those with dark hearts set out to put out His light.

And the world's rejection of Him was not an accident or an "oops" from God. As Jesus said, *"The stone which the builders rejected has become the chief cornerstone"* (Matthew 21:42). He was that rejected stone, and yet, His handling of rejection brought about His being the very stone of truth upon which all of Christianity and all of truth itself is built upon. That's the encouraging part. We have the opportunity to turn our rejection into something that we, and others, can build upon.

How did He do it? How did Jesus turn the rejection that came His way into a foundation for power and strength?

Well, first of all, He wasn't just silent, He was *peaceful* in the face of accusation He faced because He was secure in His Sonship. He knew who He was and who held Him and loved Him. When our own personal foundation is not secured in who we are in Him, we are tossed to and fro, always dependent on how others see us instead of how He sees us. That's why Paul told the Ephesians that they were to be rooted and grounded in love. We're to know the length, width, depth, and heights of His love and affection. Nothing else roots us.

He also forgave the ignorance of those around Him. They had no clue who He was and therefore He released them from the consequences of their ignorance. If we could only see that other people carry their own weaknesses and faults. Oh, we see them, but if we could see them with His eyes, we would have His compassion and would have the ability to turn a potentially destructive situation into something positive and constructive.

If we follow in Christ's footsteps in dealing with rejection, then these words from Psalm 37:23–25 will offer true, real encouragement. This psalm is about you!

> *The steps of a good man are ordered by the* Lord,
> *And He delights in his way.*
> *Though he fall, he shall not be utterly cast down;*
> *For the* Lord *upholds him with His hand.*
> *I have been young, and now am old;*
> *Yet I have not seen the righteous forsaken,*
> *Nor his descendants begging bread.*

There is no rejection from God nor will He ever forsake us. Second Corinthians 4:7–9 is a favorite passage of mine because it says just that. It constantly speaks to me right where I'm at.

But we have this treasure in earthen vessels, that the excellence of the power may be of God and not of us. We are hard-pressed on every side, yet not crushed; we are perplexed, but not in despair; persecuted, but not forsaken; struck down, but not destroyed.

Yes, we are earthen vessels, but we carry the excellence of God within us, brought forth in such a beautiful and varied array of gifts. May we realize the greatness that lies within and know that no one on this planet wants us to succeed more than our heavenly Father. He is not against you in any way, shape, or form. Just the opposite: He is your biggest fan!

3

GOD'S MASTER KEY: HUMILITY

In one *Peanuts* strip, Charlie Brown and his buddy Linus are sitting together just sharing their thoughts about what the future might hold in store for them. Linus says, "When I get big I'm going to be a humble little country doctor. I'll live in the city, see, and every morning I'll get up, climb into my sports car, and zoom into the country! Then I'll start healing people. I'll heal everybody for miles around!" He concludes his speech: "I'll be a world-famous humble little country doctor."

It's not an easy thing to remain humble. Humility is one of those attributes that we all desire but can't tell people if we've actually achieved—because that would mean we're gloating in our humility.

Although it's not easy, when growing into our gifts and callings, humility is one commodity we all need in abundance. And let's just get one thing straight right here at the beginning: humility is not weakness. There are a number of men and women I know who carry themselves with great humility but are in no way weak in body, soul, mind, or spirit.

Also, humility does not negate confidence, nor does confidence negate humility. I know that when I step up before a group of people, I am confident that God has sent me and that He is with me. I can rely on Him to fulfill His promises to me. Because I have experienced peace in His past faithfulness, I am confident of what lies ahead. There's no need to lose humility because you are confident in Him or in the gifts you've received from His hands. If you truly recognize it comes from Him, all from Him, then pride won't even get a chance to come into the picture!

In our present-day culture, however, true humility is a rare commodity. Even the term has fallen out of common usage as we instead focus on words like "relatable," "tolerant," or "inclusive." Not that such buzzwords aren't good things. But we must make sure that all we do is accomplished and rooted in humility. When we as believers begin to see ourselves according to *our gifts* as opposed to being here because of *His gift*, life begins a downward spiral.

Often people enter into their particular job, their business, or their call in life with great excitement. They usually are drawn to it with some noble purpose attached. I saw this while working as a scrub tech in a hospital surgical unit years ago. Young medical students would come into surgery wanting to share about how they were going to change the world. Some talked about taking their medical training to the furthest corners of the earth to provide medical resources for the poorest of the poor. But when they came back to the hospital a few years later as a resident, all that most of them were talking about was what they were buying next and how they were going to deal with the ever-changing insurance situations. The "change the world" language diminished quite a bit.

THE PROBLEM WITH PRIDE

When you begin to talk about humility, you do inevitably have to address its opposing force: pride. We may not have heard very many sermons on humility, but I'm sure we've all heard multiple sermons on pride. It's a popular subject because it's so easy to observe in the world around us. Between politicians, famous athletes, and celebrities, it's not hard to spot pride and its favorite first cousin…narcissism. But have we made sure that the plank has been removed from our own eye before we address the speck in another's? Let's learn from others' mistakes but not take joy in them—because that is its own specially awful kind of pride.

Listen to what the great writer and teacher C. S. Lewis said about pride in his book *Mere Christianity*:

> According to Christian teachers, the essential vice, the utmost evil, is Pride. Unchastity, anger, greed, drunkenness, and all that, are mere flea bites in comparison: it was through Pride that the devil became the devil: Pride leads to every other vice: it is the complete anti-God state of mind…. Pride…has been the chief cause of misery in every nation and every family since the world began.[2]

Wow! The "chief cause of misery in every nation and every family since the world began." Those are some pretty strong

2. C.S. Lewis, *Mere Christianity* (New York: Simon & Schuster Touchstone edition, 1996), 109, 111.

words. And yet, they are true. I've often thought that humility creates hungry students but pride creates arrogant teachers. When I find myself wanting to instruct instead of learn, I have to pull back the reins and let humility return and rule once again.

The apostle Paul addresses pride when writing to the Philippians:

> *Have this mind among yourselves, which is yours in Christ Jesus, who, though he was in the form of God, did not count equality with God a thing to be grasped, but emptied himself, by taking the form of a servant, being born in the likeness of men. And being found in human form, he humbled himself by becoming obedient to the point of death, even death on a cross.* (Philippians 2:5–8 ESV)

If there was ever a man that could glory in His gifts and power, it was Jesus. He was tempted three times by the devil; the third time with the temptation to embrace glory. Or in other words, to bathe Himself in pride. Listen to how Jesus responds to the enemy's temptation.

> *Again, the devil took Him up on an exceedingly high mountain, and showed Him all the kingdoms of the world and their glory. And he said to Him, "All these things I will give You if You will fall down and worship me." Then Jesus said to him, "Away with you, Satan! For it is written, 'You shall worship the LORD your God, and Him only you shall serve.'"* (Matthew 4:8–10)

Notice how clever the devil is. He is offering Jesus a way out—a way to avoid the cross and the hours of agony of experiencing God the Father's rejection while still receiving control over the whole world! But Jesus saw through it, as perhaps you can too. He would not allow Himself even a moment's thought of receiving all the glory of the kingdoms of this world from the devil. Jesus knew the promise of Psalm 2:8: *"Ask of Me, and I will give You the nations for Your inheritance, and the ends of the earth for Your possession."* Jesus knew the inheritance would come to Him in the Father's way and in the Father's time.

Jesus constantly is before us as the perfect example of humility. He left *the* exalted place and came to earth as a vulnerable child, relying upon simple and frail human beings, the very same human beings He Himself created. There is no greater example of pure humility.

James 4:6 reads, *"God resists the proud, but gives grace to the humble."* If we are knowingly doing something that God resists, well, something's wrong with our thinking. How can we knowingly walk down a path that will eventually encounter the resistance of the Person who created the whole world out of nothing and controls the wind, the sea, and the sky? No thanks!

HUMILITY OPENS DOORS

This chapter is meant to be a simple reminder that we are often just one step away from embracing our next promise from God. I have no desire to castigate or judge those who are wrestling with pride in their lives. Instead, I want this chapter to be more of an invitation to see the joys and benefits of walking with a humble heart. What if we had a glance of what humility could bring us? I think if we understood the doors that humility would open, we would be more open to walking in it.

The Word of God is filled with stories of people who lost something wonderful because of a spirit of pride. Cain lost his humanity by killing his brother Abel, Moses lost out on walking into the Promised Land, and Saul lost his anointing as king. Solomon, the king who had wealth, wisdom, women, and every reason to be proud, warns repeatedly in his book of Proverbs about the dangers of pride: *"When pride comes, then comes shame…"* (Proverbs 11:2) or *"By pride comes nothing but strife…"* (Proverbs 13:10) or one of the most well-known Scriptures, *"Pride goes before destruction, and a haughty spirit before a fall"* (Proverbs 16:18). Shame, strife, and destruction! Doesn't sound like a road anyone needs to travel.

On the other hand, in John 21, we have a wonderful story of humility. Now, in the previous chapter, Jesus had appeared to the disciples on a couple of occasions and also performed a number of miracles. In John 21, He comes to them again by the shore. They had gone out fishing and after a whole night they had caught nothing. Here's where it gets good. Jesus, who is not recognized at this moment, steps up and addresses the men. He says, *"Children, have you any food?"* (verse 5).

You might not think this is a big deal, but remember that Jesus is addressing grown men, men like Peter—you know, big, burly Peter who used to fish for a living. Suddenly, to them, this stranger steps up and calls them "children," which in Greek is the word *paidion*, meaning "little ones" or even "infant." He just called them little kids. The Bible doesn't describe what Peter was thinking at the time but I'm sure no grown man wants to be called a little kid. On top of that, he's got to be frustrated at a whole night of fishing and not catching anything. But, instead of reacting to Jesus' words, Peter just simply answered, "No." My, my, that doesn't sound like the Peter we meet at the beginning of the Gospel..

Now comes the zinger. Jesus doesn't leave it alone. He then says, *"Cast the net on the right side of the boat, and you will find some"* (verse 6). The boats that the disciples used were not big boats at all. They would have had to really cram everyone into one of them to travel together. From inside the boat, you can easily put one foot against one side and your other foot against the other side. This is no cruise ship they're in; it's just an itty-bitty rowboat.

Why is that important? Because Jesus just told them to move the net from the left side to the right side. I can hear one of the disciples now, "Hey, Peter, did you just hear what that guy just said? Move the net to the other side. That's like, what, five or six feet? Big difference that'll make!" But again, Peter does not argue. He could have said, "That guy doesn't know what he's talking about. If the fish aren't here, they're certainly not there!"

But he didn't. Something has changed within him. The old Peter would have argued with the stranger on the beach but the new Peter has been humbled by the events of the last few weeks. Instead of squabbling with this stranger, he does what the man says. He moves the net from one side to the other, a distance of just a few feet. A distance to an experienced fisherman that would be meaningless after hours of fishing.

But that short distance made all the difference.

Immediately the net began to fill with fish. So much so that Scripture says they couldn't haul it into the boat. They had to hold onto the net and drag it back to shore. In the middle of all this, John recognizes that the stranger on the shore is actually Jesus. Peter, so moved by his friend, jumps into the water and swims back to shore as quickly as he can. He knew where his life resided.

Peter was so close to going home empty-handed. If he had either reacted to the "children" comment or to the "move over a few feet" comment with arrogance or impatience, he wouldn't have received his provision. And it was more than a small provision. The net was filled with one hundred and fifty-three fish, large fish, more than they had ever gotten in their lives. Why? Because of humility. Their provision and the fulfillment of their livelihood was directly connected to their humble response to Jesus' instruction. What an amazing truth!

Often, the final door we need to walk through in receiving a promise is humility. In the disciples' case it came after a fruitless night when they were frustrated and exhausted. That's often the time we feel we're entitled to be more edgy and curt. And yet, it's often the final door we need to walk through to have our own personal breakthrough.

HUMILITY SHOWS GOD'S CHARACTER

One of my favorite stories in the Bible is found in 2 Kings 5. Let's introduce our main character in verse one:

Now Naaman, commander of the army of the king of Syria, was a great and honorable man in the eyes of his master, because by him the LORD had given victory to Syria. He was also a mighty man of valor, but a leper.

If you know anything about the history of the ancient Syrian army you would know one thing…they were ruthless. Known for their ferocity in battle, the man in charge of this war machine must have been an incredible fighter and skilled in strategy as well as brave. His name, as we see, was Naaman. In spite of his leprosy, he remained commander, for he was a man of valor, loved and honored by the king. However, one can only imagine how devastated Naaman—used to being respected and strong—was by an illness that gradually ate away at his skin.

A young girl from Israel had been enslaved and was now the servant of Naaman's wife. She told Naaman's wife about a man in Israel who had the power of God to heal. This was relayed to the king of Syria and eventually made its way to the king of Israel. Thinking that he was being manipulated, the king of Israel tore his clothes and declared himself unable to heal.

Elisha heard about it and instructed the king of Israel to send Naaman to him. Elisha knew where healing came from.

Now, imagine that you're Naaman. You've got leprosy and you just found out that a prophet of God has said that if you go to him, you will be healed. He must have been so excited. He gathered together a group of men, with servants, chariots, and gifts, and made his way to the door of Elisha. Standing at the door of an unassuming little dwelling place, he summoned Elisha—but rather than a prophet who bows and respects his position, Naaman just gets Elisha's servant instead. Taking a bit of biblical liberty, I see it going like this:

"Who are you, young man?"

"Oh, hi, I'm Bobby. You must be Mr. Naaman."

"Yes, I am. Where is your master?"

"Ah, he's inside. He told me to tell you to go down to the Jordan River and dunk up and down seven times and you'll be healed."

"What! Never! Bring out the prophet...right now!"

"Ah...I don't think that's gonna happen. He's pretty busy. You know, prophet things and such. But, if you'll go down to the river...."

"I heard you, I heard you! I certainly didn't expect this."

Naaman had seen it going quite differently. He had thought to himself, *"He will surely come out to me, and stand and call on the name of the LORD his God, and wave his hand over the place, and heal the leprosy"* (2 Kings 5:11).

(Sounds to me like Naaman's been to a few modern healing services.)

Instead of heeding the advice, Naaman turned away in a rage and started down the road back to Syria, only to be stopped by one of his trusted servants who was obviously a man who understood the power of humility. I love the gentleness and honor in which the servant approaches his master Naaman: *"My father, if the prophet had told you to do something great, would you not have done it? How much more then, when he says to you, 'Wash, and be clean'?"* (2 Kings 5:13).

This is the moment of truth. When we are expecting something good but it seems to be coming to us in an unorthodox manor, or even a way that appears weak and foolish, how do we respond? If Elisha had come out and told Naaman to climb a mountain backwards, he probably would have done it. Instead, he is told to go to a dirty, muddy, shallow river and dunk up and down seven times. What Elisha is really telling him to do is to go to the river and act like a little child, because that's what kids do, they jump up and down in water and dunk themselves over and over. God, through Elisha, was inviting Naaman to become as a child. Jesus used similar words with Peter and the disciples.

DESPERATION IS A TRAIT THAT COMES IN HANDY WHEN GOD IS ASKING YOU TO DO SOMETHING CRAZY, SOMETHING YOU THINK YOU'RE TOO DIGNIFIED TO DO.

So, does Naaman do it? Would we do it? I wonder how many times we have been invited into a place of healing only to be diverted away because of the form in which it came to us. Naaman was desperate, though. Desperation is a trait that comes in handy when God is asking you to do something crazy, something you think you're too dignified to do.

So Naaman takes his servant's advice and heads to the river. Imagine how he must have felt to begin a process where every step you take is one of humility, even childlikeness. But desperation spurred him on. It must have been something for the men with him to see their strong and prideful commander going into the river, ready to dunk himself over and over. I'm sure Naaman was watching them watch him. He must have felt foolish, and yet, with humility comes hope. They are tied together.

I wonder if he checked himself for healing every time he came up out of the water. I probably would have, at least the first couple of times. But he pressed on and, obeying the word of the prophet, dunked seven times. When he came up after the seventh time, the Scripture says, *"his flesh was restored like the flesh of a little child, and he was clean"* (2 Kings 5:14). His flesh now mirrored his childlike humility.

The first thing Naaman does after that is go back to Elisha and attempt to give him a gift. Elisha won't take it because he knows it was not his power but the power of God that healed Naaman. And it seems that Naaman understands because he makes this incredible statement: *"Indeed, now I know that there is no God in all the earth, except in Israel…"* (verse 15).

That's what humility did for Naaman. It not only allowed him to see the power of God, but also that this God was the true God. His humility continues as he asks Elisha for grace as he is now headed back to a world of idols and false gods. He asks Elisha for forgiveness when he has to go with the king into the Temple of Rimmon. He now knows who the real God is but he is still a man under authority and he wants to know if God will pardon him as he humbly serves the king of Syria.

This is amazing. All manner of pride seems to have vanished from Naaman. He's like a small child asking for help. "Elisha, what should I do when I get home? I need to serve the king but

I don't believe in those gods anymore. Would you and your God absolve me when I am in the temple serving my king?" Elisha simply responds with, "*Go in peace*" (verse 19).

What a beautiful story of hope, forgiveness, healing, and humility. All those doors opened up for Naaman because he first embraced humility. Imagine if we would embrace humility as a lifestyle as opposed to pursuing our own life goals or ministry goals. What would we learn about God?

HUMILITY AND YOU

A few years ago, an ESPN poll identified Tim Tebow as America's most popular athlete. What was so ironic about his sports stardom, of course, is that Tebow was not always a success as an NFL quarterback. And he knew it. When giving interviews he would always talk about his mistakes, even when the reporters were trying to get him to talk about his successes. If he was talking about success on the field, he would always direct his praise to his team and to specific teammates. His response to the ESPN poll was exactly what you'd think it would be... humble. He said, "It tells me they have a lot of crazy polls out there. I hope people see I'm real and genuine. I hope they see that I make a ton of mistakes but that I always get back up and try again."[3]

The real test of his humility came when, after a dissatisfying career in the NFL, Tim Tebow switched sports to play minor league baseball. For an athlete to change careers like that takes either an astonishingly huge ego or an amazing capacity for humility. I'd argue that with Tebow, it's the latter. Some sports fans are lining up to buy his jersey. Others, like one ESPN sports commentator, are almost in awe of his audacity in the

3. Quoted in Jeremie Kubicek, "3 Examples of Everyday Humble Leaders," JeremieKubicek.com, http://jeremiekubicek.com/3-examples-of-everyday-humble-leaders/ (accessed June 2, 2017).

face of inevitable failure: "What continues to make him one of the most puzzling and compelling athletes of his era, though, is not the long string of embarrassments, but rather, what seems to be Tebow's absolute fearlessness in the face of…a challenge that is almost certainly going to be his greatest, most public humiliation yet."[4]

Why would Tebow continue on despite such virulent—and one dares to say, well-founded—critics? Maybe, just maybe, because he has this otherworldly capacity, so rare especially in the sports world. Maybe, just maybe, it's because he's humble, both in church and on the field.

Are we able to carry humility into all areas of our lives in a similar way?

It's not just the church that thrives when humility is in place. Our homes as well as our workplaces all find growth when we walk in a humble manner. In a recent article in the *Harvard Business Review*, the number one factor cited for creating an environment where employees flourish is none other than our good friend, humility. That's right. The importance of leading with humility and responding to direction with humility was reported as the biggest contributing factor to an environment where people can innovate and bring needed growth to their company.[5] When bosses directed their employees with a humble heart, employees found themselves wanting to not only do a good job, but to surprise their bosses by doing a great job. When bosses saw humility in their employees, a greater trust was built between them resulting in releasing to the employee

---

4. David Fleming, "Tim Tebow's relentless pursuit of failure," *ESPN*, March 1, 2017, http://www.espn.com/mlb/story/_/id/18791367/tim-tebow-relentless-pursuit-failure (accessed May 4, 2017).

5. See Jeanine Prime and Elizabeth Salib, "The Best Leaders Are Humble Leaders," *Harvard Business Review*, May 12, 2014, https://hbr.org/2014/05/the-best-leaders-are-humble-leaders (accessed June 2, 2017).

even greater responsibility and new opportunities. It works both ways.

Who would you rather work with: a coworker who's gifted yet arrogant or one who's still- learning but hard-working and humble? And how do you present yourself? If you feel good about how you perform in an area, do people see a confident yet modest person or do they see someone who carries around a pretentious and smug demeanor? I know that I would rather partner with a humble learner than a gifted egotist.

Micah 6:8 invites us to this higher (lower?) life. God says to us very simply, *"He has shown you, O man, what is good; and what does the LORD require of you but to do justly, to love mercy, and to **walk humbly** with your God?"*

That's pretty basic. Walk with God, and man, in a humble manner. Peter received his provision, a literal boat-load of fish, because he responded to a stranger with humility. Naaman embraced humility and found not only healing but the character of God. Imagine what might await us if we will carry His heart and walk as He walked! The world is hungry for people who live with an air of humility. When you do, it will open doors you would never expect—and just may lead you out of your stuck situation.

4

LIVING OUTSIDE THE COMFORT ZONE

They say that one of the hardest things to do in sports is to hit a ball thrown by a major league pitcher. I've never had the opportunity to find that out from experience, but I've always wanted to give it a try. (Any major league pitcher out there want to give me a shot?)

But if hitting a pitch wasn't hard enough, imagine being a pinch hitter. Not a designated hitter like they have in the American League, but a pinch hitter. For those who don't know, a designated hitter is a regular in the lineup. Though he doesn't play the field, he can prepare for his "at bat" because he knows who is batting before him. The pinch hitter is a different animal altogether. He's the guy who has been sitting it out the whole game, watching it in all the comfort of the team bench, until he's called in by the coach.

Sounds fine, right? Now imagine what it must be like to be sitting there when suddenly the manager looks your way and calls your name. You haven't warmed up yet and your body lets you know it the moment you stand. To top that off, your cold body is about ready to meet the opposing team's red-hot pitcher. Even worse, it's usually their closer, the guy who specializes in getting three quick outs to end the game.

That is the world of the pinch hitter and nobody did it better than Matt Stairs. During nearly twenty years in the Majors, Stairs played for twelve teams. He began as a starter but over the years he became known as baseball's greatest pinch hitter. During his career, he had a .252 batting average and a .833 OPS percentage, which is the sum of a player's on-base percentage and slugging average. Incredibly, he hit a home run every 18 at-bats and knocked in a run every 4.78 at-bats. To put that in perspective, the 2015 batting average for MLB pinch hitters was only .220. Again, Stair's batting average was .252, and that was over many years.

Stairs' most memorable moment came in Game 4 of the 2008 National League Championship Series. With his team behind, he came off the bench as a pinch-hitter and helped the Phillies win the game on their way to the World Series.

Isn't that what so many little kids dream of? There they are, waiting for their moment, when suddenly they're called upon to come and do the seemingly impossible.

When the coach says, "Chris, you're up," what would my response be?

"Ah, Coach, I'm actually not ready yet. Can I go to the bathroom and maybe get a snack before I go out there?"

"No, you're up!"

"But Coach, I'm not mentally prepared for what's about to happen. I didn't visualize this moment as being like this. Can you just give me a few minutes?"

"No, you're up!"

"Coach, I appreciate the opportunity, believe me. The thing is, I'm not completely sure I'm ready. Plus, their pitcher has a really mean curve ball and I don't do well when curves are thrown my way. You know what I mean?"

"Oh, yeah, I know exactly what you mean, but don't worry, you're no longer up!"

READY OR NOT...

Often, and I don't know why, God presents us with the most incredible opportunities when we're not feeling fully prepared. This chapter is not addressing a specific weakness per se. Instead, it's focusing on what most of us may feel at one time or another: "I'm not ready!"

Paul makes a beautiful statement in Ephesians 2:10: *"For we are His workmanship, created in Christ Jesus for good works, which God prepared beforehand that we should walk in them."* We have been created to walk in some amazing and wonderful works that God prepared for us. What an incredible truth! What God doesn't always tell us, though, is precisely *what* works He's planned for us, or exactly what the path will look like.

Sometimes it feels like God is calling out, "ready, *fire,* aim." Instead of giving you time to aim and fully prepare your big shot, God takes away your moment to settle in. You end up becoming prepared while you're in the middle of the doing.

Putting yourself out there, even when you do feel ready, is scary enough. But when you feel ill-prepared for the task, it takes on a whole new feeling. Especially when it comes out of left field or with the "suddenly" that takes you off the bench.

Second Timothy 4:2 says, *"Be ready in season and out of season…."* Though that verse is directly related to having the Word in us so that we are ready to share love and truth with anyone at any time, it is also a wonderful encouragement to those of us who are invited by God to step outside our secure and safe box to give out the life that lives within us.

Living safely has many meanings. Some are good, and some…not so good. I'm a father and a grandfather. I want my kids and my grandkids to be safe at all times, but I've learned over the years that I can only do so much to make that happen. Some parents only pass on their own fears to their children. "Don't touch that! Don't eat that! Don't swing so high!" If "don't" is a significant part of every outing or new experience, those children become more concerned with what *not* to do instead of learning what they're actually *capable* of doing. So, I tried to pass along wisdom to my kids that they could pass along to their kids on how to walk though this life with a degree of caution but never timidity. It requires a mixture of wisdom as well as stretching them into believing they can do even more than they ever realized or dreamed.

LIVING OUR DREAMS NEVER COMES WITHOUT PAIN AND HEARTACHE.

Discreetly engaging life's challenges produces wise learners as well as confident overcomers. Fear-based living, on the other hand, produces a tentativeness that creates a shield around a person. They may call it a protective shield, but in reality it's not. It's a restrictive cage, a self-made prison that allows them to watch from the sidelines while others are living their dreams. Living our dreams never comes without pain and heartache, but as we look to Him, the author and finisher of our faith, we find ourselves with a grace to press through the pain and the heartache.

LIVING OUR PLANS OR LIVING HIS PLANS

Wouldn't it be nice if we could plan our lives like we plan a day?

My day: "I'll get up at 7:00 a.m., take care of my morning activities and at 8:00 I'll eat my breakfast. I'll then kiss my wife at 8:25 and head out the door and start work at my desk at 9:00 sharp. At 11:00 I'll take my 15-minute break…"etc.

My life: "I'll graduate with honors and then go to college for four years and get my degree. I won't look at a woman until I get my master's degree. Then I'll marry the most beautiful woman in the world and after three years we'll start having our three children: a girl, a boy, and then another girl, each being three years apart. When they're all in school…"etc.

I know, it sounds pretty ridiculous when you write it out like that, yet for many, unfulfilled plans are daily causing them tremendous frustration and stress. But if we could see it from God's perspective, we would see that frustrated plans are actually a potential opportunity for growth, maturing, enlargement, and often…advancement.

When I was a kid going through growth spurts, I had, like all little kids before and after me, growing pains. The pain and throbbing in my legs was especially distressing. Nighttime was downright uncomfortable. (To help, my father would give me his "compression socks," which were really just his ankle socks that would cover up my whole leg and somehow make me feel better.) My growth spurts taught me that stretching will often bring discomfort. If we live our lives always trying to separate ourselves from discomfort, we will only stunt our growth.

Brown Bannister, a dear friend of mine, has been a producer in the Contemporary Christian music world for decades. As of this writing, he has won twenty-five Dove awards, fourteen Grammy awards, and has been inducted into the Gospel Music Hall of Fame. Not bad for a guy who was thrust into the business, as he says, before his time. Over dinner one day he told me the story and it's stuck with me for years.

Brown's father had told him that he wasn't cut out for music. As a matter of fact, his father said, instead of being a musician, Brown had the skill and temperament to be a mortician. A mortician! Never! But, before any money was invested in college, his dad asked him to take an aptitude, skills, and personality test to see what he actually qualified for. Much to Brown's amazement, when the results came back they said that the perfect job for him would be—you guessed it—a mortician!

In spite of parental advice and personality tests, Brown enrolled at Belmont University in Nashville. He loved music and looked forward to his time at college to learn the behind-the-scenes world of music recording so that maybe, someday, he would be able to do it for a living. He was just a few weeks into his first semester as a freshman when he received a call from a friend, Chris Christian. Chris asked Brown to help him with a recording project for which he had been recently hired. Chris's role was to produce a new project for B. J. Thomas, a very successful singer at the time. He had a hit record a few years earlier with a song called "Raindrops Keep Falling on My Head" but wanted to get back to his Christian roots with an album that would eventually be titled *Home Where I Belong*.

Brown asked Chris what his role would be. Chris said, "Oh, I'll need you as my recording engineer."

"Recording engineer! I haven't even had a class on how to plug in microphones yet!"

But Chris told him not to worry. He knew Brown and he knew his capacity to learn. Plus, he knew his character and Brown's sincere love for God. Chris trusted that he also had an immense heart and all the humility one needed to learn something new.

After some wrangling, Brown finally acquiesced and took the job. Feeling utterly unqualified and insecure, Brown walked into the recording studio that first day and looked around. There before him were first-class studio instrumentalists, ready to begin their next project. Fortunately, mics were in place and his job was just to get behind the console and do a sound check. A guitar player asked Brown if he would tweak the sound of his guitar. Brown said sure and then looked down at the board. There before him was the largest soundboard he had ever seen. It looked like the console of a spaceship.

He noticed that it was numbered and figured that each number must be a separate line out to a specific vocal mic or instrument. He found one labeled "guitar" but then he noticed all the various knobs lined up above it. *What do all these things do?* Assuming that they must affect the sound somehow, he began to play with them, turning them this way and that, hoping that it would bring about the desired change. At the same time he was *"praying without ceasing,"* crying out for God's help. What a great combo; the bravery to stick your neck out into the unknown and the humility to ask God for His grace and wisdom in the midst of it.

Suddenly he heard a voice from the other room. It was the guitar player. Brown instantly thought to himself, *Oh, no, here we go. This could be my most short-lived job ever.* But instead he heard something totally unexpected. The voice quietly and sweetly said, "Hey, man, that's perfect. Thank you." Brown smiled, turned his back to the guy, and then began to slowly slump to the ground. He sat there on that cold studio floor and prayed, *God, thank you, but you've really got to help me with all this.*

And help him He did. *Home Where I Belong* won a Grammy for Best Gospel/Inspirational Recording and went on to become a Gold Record. Not bad for a first-time effort. If that wasn't enough, Chris then contacted him again. Chris had been asked to produce a young female artist but didn't have time with all his other obligations. So, he did what he knew would work. He asked Brown to produce it.

Brown's response was simple, "What? I've never produced anything in my life! I'm thinking that's not the best idea." Chris countered with, "Well, do what I just did. You watched me produce an album, you just do the same thing." After much going back and forth, Brown accepted the challenge and worked with a young gal to produce her first album. It was a self-titled album called *Amy Grant*. It did pretty well.

Brown would go on to produce the next fourteen Amy Grant albums. Her fourth, *Age to Age*, became the first Christian album by a solo artist to be certified gold (1983), and a couple of years later, the first Christian album to be certified platinum. It became so popular that it topped Billboard's Christian albums chart for eighty-five weeks, and was named Gospel Album of the 1980s by *Billboard Magazine*. He also recorded her beloved Christmas albums, which to this day still fill our house each Christmas season with beauty, grace, and joy.

It all would have been different if Brown had told Chris, "You know, I appreciate that you thought of me, but I've never done anything like that and I'm not sure I'd do a good enough job. As a matter of fact, I'm sure I would just embarrass myself, as well as you. I hope you don't mind but I think I'll sit this one out." I, for one, am so glad that he didn't "sit this one out." For years, when Christmastime approached and we would put on Amy's albums, I would call Brown and thank him for doing what he does so well.

A funny thing happened in our country over the last century. For centuries previously, people learned through a combination of learned educators and hands-on experience. Over the last century, however, learning has become more classroom-oriented, morphing into huge lecture rooms filled with listening, semi-listening, and semi-sleeping students. Over the last two decades it has been mingled with online opportunities giving students multiple choices in how they want to approach their education.

Despite the increase in opportunities, what seems to be missing in so many lives today is an opportunity to learn "while doing." So much of our learning today is cognitive learning, centering on intellectual, cerebral, and emotional scholarship, as opposed to a primarily experiential form of learning. They are both good and necessary, but when you remove hands-on training from someone's life, the horse of inexperience is always pulling the cart of giftings. This can make for some wonderfully gifted but inexperienced, timid, and intimidated people.

Are you one?

BEFORE HIS TIME?

There's one guy who always comes to mind when I think of being thrust into a role "before it's time," and that would be Jesus. You know the story, but here it is again from John 2:

On the third day there was a wedding in Cana of Galilee, and the mother of Jesus was there. Now both Jesus and His disciples were invited to the wedding. And when they ran out of wine, the mother of Jesus said to Him, "They have no wine."

Jesus said to her, "Woman, what does your concern have to do with Me? My hour has not yet come."

His mother said to the servants, "Whatever He says to you, do it."

Now there were set there six waterpots of stone, according to the manner of purification of the Jews, containing twenty or thirty gallons apiece. Jesus said to them, "Fill the waterpots with water." And they filled them up to the brim. And He said to them, "Draw some out now, and take it to the master of the feast." And they took it. When the master of the feast had tasted the water that was made wine, and did not know where it came from (but the servants who had drawn the water knew), the master of the feast called the bridegroom. And he said to him, "Every man at the beginning sets out the good wine, and when the guests have well drunk, then the inferior. You have kept the good wine until now!"

This beginning of signs Jesus did in Cana of Galilee, and manifested His glory; and His disciples believed in Him.

(John 2:1–11)

God allowed His Son to experience what we experience on a regular basis, that is, movement into your callings and gifts even before you have made all your plans. A call to your destiny when you feel it's not your time.

I know that Jesus was aware of everything happening around Him. He wasn't thrown by His mother's question. He didn't ask "How does this concern me?" because He didn't know the answer. He knew quite well, but by so doing He gave us a perfect example of stepping out when you're called upon, even out of season, and then expecting God to come through. I don't think we realize how often God is waiting to bring honor to Himself through our lack of planning, perfecting, and control. He truly gets the glory when we think we're not ready.

I'm no longer in my twenties, my thirties, my forties, or even my fifties. I can't get back time but I can make the best use of the time that God still allows me to breathe. Until that last breath I want to have a heart that says "yes." Yes to trying new things, yes to finishing up some old things, and yes to learning as I go as opposed to always having to learn before I go.

Let Timothy say it one more time. He says in 2 Timothy 4:2, *"Be ready in season and out of season."*

Ah...in season! That's when everything is going great and you feel in total control of your destiny. You are like a master chef preparing a meal with all the finest ingredients neatly laid out before you. You're at peace with yourself and the world because you, my friend, are "in your wheelhouse." They are the moments that we get to showcase our gifts and talents.

Ah...out of season! That's when you get a last minute phone call telling you that the mayor will be at your house in one hour, expecting an exquisite dinner. You rush into the kitchen only to find it in total disarray. As you search for the ingredients to your favorite "quick meal," you find that they are not there. But you do have all the ingredients for a dish you've never made. You have a choice: bail on the whole thing or begin to cook up something new using unfamiliar or even strange new ingredients. These are the moments that we are stretched, and in the process we are given the opportunity to grow.

LIVING OUT OF THE BOX

I have been writing and playing music for over forty years. I love watching a new song come to life. Sometimes you know where the song is going, but other times it seems to take you in a completely different direction. As a result, I have a number of songs that just would not fit in your basic Christian worship album. I've been contemplating, once my current music project is done, gathering all these atypical songs together on one album and calling it *Out of the Box*.

A box is made to carry things, not to live in. It may start out as being a place of protecting valuable things, but if those things are left inside, it becomes their permanent holding place—or worse, a place where things are forgotten. Have you ever moved and then a year or so later found a box that you'd forgotten about? When you opened it you discovered all these wonderful new treasures. Treasures that you had completely forgotten about because you couldn't see them for the cardboard.

So many people allow themselves to remain in some sort of "safe place," thinking that it's the wise thing to do, when in reality, they are allowing themselves to be put in a place where they will be at first overlooked, and then eventually forgotten. If we continually say "no" to everything new that comes our way and then feel "stuck," we have no one to blame but ourselves.

When we are given an opportunity to spread our wings, especially when it's been a heart's desire, don't bow to fear of the unknown. It's only unknown until you know it. Then, when you do, you end up owning it.

It's a funny thing, stepping outside the box. When you finally do, you gain a whole new set of glasses. Glasses that not only let you see new possibilities and options, but that let you see and meet new people who have been living outside the box for years.

What's that thing in front of you labeled *Out of the Box*? Is it starting a new business, going back to school to finish your degree, or finally starting to write that book you've been talking about for years? I was challenged to write a book but I hemmed and hawed. I found every good reason not to do it and for a time I didn't. Someone once asked me, "Do you know the difference between someone who writes a book and someone who doesn't write a book?" I answered, "No." They responded with a chuckle, "The person that writes the book, writes the book!" That floored me. It was simple. Just start! Don't worry about the ten thousandth word, just worry about the next sentence.

Probably the greatest biblical example to this concept of moving outside the box is found in Matthew 14. The disciples see a figure on the water and cry out in fear, *"It's a ghost!"* Of course, it's Jesus, and He speaks to them and tries to calm them down, but Peter is still not convinced it's Him. He challenges, *"Lord, if it is You, command me to come to You on the water."* Notice he didn't say, "in the water," he said, *"on the water."* Jesus simple said, *"Come"* (verses 28–29).

WHEN WE ARE GIVEN AN OPPORTUNITY TO SPREAD OUR WINGS, ESPECIALLY WHEN IT'S BEEN A HEART'S DESIRE, DON'T BOW TO FEAR OF THE UNKNOWN.

We all know what happened next. Peter stepped out, took a few steps, became fearful of the storm and, taking his eyes off Jesus, began to sink. Jesus took his hand and walked him to the boat. Most people get caught up in the fact that Peter sank because he took his eyes off Jesus. What I'm amazed at is this: there are only two people in history that have ever walked on water, Jesus and Peter. None of the other disciples asked Jesus if they could walk on the water. Peter saw an opportunity to step out of his comfort zone and walk on the water with God. You gotta love the guy for that!

Even to this day, the expression, "stepping out of the boat" means to try walking into something new and uncharted. Not everything in life comes with a perfect plan. That's why in Acts 17:28 it says, *"In Him we live and move and have our being."* He is waiting on the water for us to step out. Storms may come but He is there. Waves may crash but He is there. To most people water is for drinking. For some, though, it's an invitation to go for a walk.

I'll see you outside the box!

AGE DOESN'T MATTER (UNLESS YOU'RE CHEESE)

Can you imagine starting out life with not one name, not three names, but five—including Johannes, Chrysostomus, and Theophilus? Why mom and dad, why? Such was the beginning of this young boy from Central Europe.

He was the youngest of seven children, five of whom died in infancy. His older sister was a musical prodigy and at the age of three he would spend countless hours watching and listening while their father gave her lessons at the keyboard. The young boy was a quick learner. By the time he was four years old he was playing minuets on the clavier and by the age of five he was composing his own musical compositions. At eight he wrote his first symphony.

Just to be clear, a symphony is not a "longer song" as some-one once said. Here's the dictionary definition: "A symphony is an elaborate instrumental composition in three or more move-ments, similar in form to a sonata but written for an orches-tra and usually of far grander proportions and more varied elements."

At *eight years old* he was writing music for every single instru-ment within the orchestra! At age eight I was learning how to play "Chopsticks." At eight years old he could play multiple instruments. At eight I was playing with a Frisbee. A symphony usually has three movements, each a unique part that fits into the whole. At age eight, my greatest movement was my ability to suddenly become still while playing freeze tag.

I'm sure by now you're all aware that I've been talking about Mozart, or to be more precise, Johannes Chrysostomus Wolfgangus Theophilus Mozart. Kinda flows right off the tongue, doesn't it?

No one told him he couldn't do something because he was too young. Can you imagine if his father had said, "Hey, son, put that violin down. You're much too young to be playing with that. It's your sister's time right now. Your time will come sooner or later." If he had, we may never have known the genius of Mozart.

THE GIFT IS WITHIN YOU

"Your time will come…." What if Paul had said that to Timothy? "Timothy, my son, what do you think you're doing trying to help your mother with the church and all the highly spiritual things she's dealing with? You're much too young and immature. Just sit tight a little longer and get some more wisdom and maybe someday you'll have your chance. Remember, Jesus waited till He was thirty years old. If He waited till then, you should probably wait till you're thirty-five or forty."

Fortunately, we all know that Paul didn't say that. Instead, he told Timothy in 1 Timothy 4:12–14, *"Let no one despise your youth, but be an example to the believers in word, in conduct, in love, in spirit, in faith, in purity. Till I come, give attention to reading, to exhortation, to doctrine. Do not neglect the gift that is in you, which was given to you by prophecy with the laying on of the hands of the eldership."*

"Let no one despise your youth." I love that! I was saved at nineteen and was immediately ushered into a world of receiving and giving. It was expected that you would attend Bible studies and be a person of prayer as well as worship. The four heart standards of the day were worship, Bible study, fellowship, and prayer. It was the Jesus Movement and we were all college-age kids still being kids, of course, yet at the same time, earnestly seeking God. No one told us we were too young. On the contrary, we were encouraged to try everything.

Like Paul's admonition to Timothy, we were instructed to make sure that more was going into us than what was coming out of us. Paul makes it very clear that Timothy was to walk in love, purity, faith, and biblical study. He also highlighted one other thing. Paul told him that he was a gifted man and that he needed to make sure that he did not neglect the gifts within him. It's clear in the first chapter of 2 Timothy that Timothy needed encouragement to walk with confidence in his gifts from God.

How many people have had their gifts neglected and shut down because someone didn't fully see them? How many of us have only seen someone's age, education, or experience, instead of their gifts? Now, I totally understand that we need to have wisdom when we're in a position to release people into places of leadership or influence. I wouldn't put an eight-year-old in the driver's seat of a bus. Yet, I would be happy to have an eight-year-old who loves Jesus pray for me. I've received some of the sweetest and most authentic prayers from little ones.

I remember when I was in junior high, the teacher asked the class what we would like to be when we grew up. We were a small farming community so most of the kids went through the normal occupations of the day such as fireman, teacher, farmer, etc. I had been a political junkie since I was a little kid. I memorized the presidents when I was four years old and used to sneak out from my bedroom when I was six so I could watch the Kennedy/Nixon debates. Thanks to those escapades, I had more lofty goals in mind. I boldly told my teacher that I wanted to become the President of the United States. Some kids chuckled quietly, which neither surprised nor bothered me. Then suddenly one of the kids said, "That's the stupidest thing I've ever heard. DuPré, there's no way *you* could ever become president." Instantly the class erupted with laughter and I sat there, frozen—I told you how well I could freeze while playing freeze tag. The teacher saw my embarrassment and quickly moved on to the next kid. But that one moment of laughter shut me down and I never voiced anything like that again.

This might not be a perfect example of the older shutting down the younger, but it is a very personal example for me of what happens in the heart of the young when their dreams are laughed at, derided, or even ignored. It can actually remove the dream from their heart. Sadly for me and for our country, I never became president.

But seriously, something funny happened to all the Baby Boomer kids who took over the Jesus Movement. Our generation was handed the baton when we were in our early twenties but we have kept holding on to it well into our fifties, our sixties, and even into our seventies. We think, *Well, we need to be wise and raise up people who are mature and who have some of life's issues already worked out in their lives.*

Really? Is that how it worked for us? Did we have all of our issues worked out before we stepped into positions of leadership or influence?

I sure didn't, but because I was faithful with what was before me, He was faithful to mature me, guide me, and allow me to fail.

Fear of failure has been the quiet excuse for many older leaders to withhold releasing authority to a younger generation. But that is nowhere near a good enough reason. Of course they'll fail. At some time during their tenure they will fail. Who doesn't fail?

Thank God for Psalm 37:23–24. Look at this:

The steps of a good man are ordered by the LORD,
And He delights in his way.
Though he fall, he shall not be utterly cast down;
For the LORD upholds him with His hand.

FEAR OF FAILURE HAS BEEN THE QUIET EXCUSE FOR MANY OLDER LEADERS TO WITHHOLD RELEASING AUTHORITY TO A YOUNGER GENERATION.

The thing is, God knows we will eventually fail at something. Sometimes we fail on a regular basis. Even when our steps are ordered by the Lord, they are still walked out by very ordinary human beings. But falling and being utterly cast down are two different things. His ability to uphold us in the midst of our weakness and failure is both humbling and something to cherish.

Do those around us feel that we will uphold them when they fall or fail? Do people feel they have to behave around us in order to belong or do we make people feel as if they "belong" even while they're learning how to "behave"?

Risking nothing produces exactly that, nothing. Failure is not the end. It's actually one of the rewards of trying. I don't know anyone who has never failed. It's not failing that worries me, it's the not trying. I remember hearing a gifted athlete being interviewed after great victory. He was asked if this was the most important moment of his career. He said, "No. The most important moment of my career was when I took my first few steps."

For many people, as they look back on their lives, the biggest regrets are not the things that they did, but the things they never attempted, for whatever reason. I know so many adults who wish they could play piano or guitar. Guess what, it's not too late! A year from now you could be doing something you've always wanted to do. Go for it! Step out! You're not too old and you're not too late. With two one hour lessons a month, a year from now you could be playing beautiful music on your keyboard or guitar. And as we all know as you get older, a year is such a short time. Redeem it! You'll be forever grateful.

TOO YOUNG?

Just to encourage those younger hearts that are reading this book, here are a few people whom God thought were qualified to lead at an early age.

Joseph was seventeen years old when he was sold to Potiphar and was quickly put in charge of Potiphar's household:

Now Joseph had been brought down to Egypt, and Potiphar, an officer of Pharaoh, the captain of the guard, an Egyptian, had bought him from the Ishmaelites who had brought him down there. The Lord was with Joseph, and he became a successful man, and he was in the house of his Egyptian master. His master saw that the Lord was with him and that the Lord caused all that he did to succeed in his hands. So Joseph found favor in his sight and attended him, and he made him overseer of his house and put him in charge of all that he had.   (Genesis 39:1–4 ESV)

Josiah was eight years old when he became king in Jerusalem:

Josiah was eight years old when he began to reign, and he reigned thirty-one years in Jerusalem. And he did what was right in the eyes of the Lord, and walked in the ways of David his father; and he did not turn aside to the right hand or to the left.   (2 Chronicles 34:1–2 ESV)

Mary of Nazareth was a young virgin when she conceived the Savior, Jesus.

In the sixth month the angel Gabriel was sent from God to a city of Galilee named Nazareth, to a virgin betrothed to a man whose name was Joseph, of the house of David. And the virgin's name was Mary. And he came to her and said, "Greetings, O favored one, the Lord is with you!" But she was greatly troubled at the saying, and tried to discern what sort of greeting this might be. And the angel said to her, "Do not be afraid, Mary, for you have found favor with God. And behold, you will conceive in your womb and bear a son, and you shall call his name Jesus. He will be great and will be called the Son of the Most High. And the Lord God will give to him the throne of his father David, and he will reign

over the house of Jacob forever, and of his kingdom there will
be no end."   (Luke 1:26–33 ESV)

If we only looked at their ages and said, "Why can't I be in charge? They were. Why aren't I given the same kinds of responsibilities that Joseph was given? What's wrong with me?" then we would be missing the bigger picture. Each one of the above examples is of people who, at an early and tender age, had lived their short lives for Him and Him alone. Joseph learned his lesson quickly and set out to apply his gifts in a humble way, honoring others at every turn. Josiah, though only eight years old when he became king, did not turn to the right or the left. He set his eyes on God and never looked back. And Mary, well, what more can be said of this amazing woman of God? She showed her devotion to God and embraced what was right by being willing to appear wrong.

The challenge, then, for you who are younger, is to not focus on your gifts being recognized, but rather focus on having your character shine through in everything you do. It's then that your gifts become more sought after, even more desirable.

As Peter says in 1 Peter 5:5, "*You younger men, likewise… clothe yourselves with humility toward one another, for God is opposed to the proud but gives grace to the humble*" (NASB).

May there be a flood of humble and gifted young leaders, both men and women, who rise up in the days ahead!

TOO OLD?

It's not just the younger ones who often feel displaced. Some hit the ground running at an early age, but for most of the rest of us, it happens later in life.

One man, elected twice as the leader of his country, was hardly an overachiever when he was young. He continually fell short throughout his early years at school, eventually failing the sixth grade. Though one day he would win a Nobel Peace Prize, he went year after year winning nothing and failing miserably, especially in his career as a politician. He was defeated in every election for public office until the age of sixty-two when he won his first election...for Prime Minister of the United Kingdom.

Without Winston Churchill's leadership, it's not certain whether England would have been able to withstand the onslaught from Hitler and the Third Reich. Churchill was the right man at the right time. He galvanized the people of England, not only awakening them to the puissance and power of their enemy, but also giving them the courage to both endure and fight. And fight they did, defeating Germany in the Battle of Britain in 1940. Had Hitler won that battle, it's almost certain England would have fallen to the Nazis. Thank God that this "older man" stepped forward.

Have you ever tried to get a job after turning forty? How about after turning fifty, or sixty? I think the conversation people or companies have with those of us who sport a little (or a lot) of gray hair goes something like this:

(Interviewer): "I'm so sorry. You seem absolutely wonderful and we appreciate all your experience, but we won't be able to use you at this time."

(Gray-haired wise person): "Why is that?"

(Interviewer): "Well, believe it or not, you're over-qualified."

(Gray-haired wise person): "I'm sorry...over-qualified?"

(Interviewer): "You're too old!"

Here's the thing, God didn't just call Moses at the ripe old age of eighty to free the Israelites from bondage. God actually *waited* for Moses to turn eighty before He spoke to him about the job ahead. Why did He wait till then? Why didn't God have

Moses lead the Israelites out of Egypt when he was younger and stronger?

Because sometimes younger and stronger aren't the most suitable ingredients that are needed for a particular job. Certain tasks require someone who has more wisdom than self-confidence. I'm sure that a forty-year-old Moses would have handled things differently than the eighty-year-old Moses did. As it was, even at eighty he had such fiery anger and impatience with the Israelites that he struck the rock twice in frustration and ended up being barred from entering the Promised Land. Imagine what kind of emotions would have been directed toward the people of Israel had a forty-year-old Moses led them forth! Who knows what else, or who else, he might have hit with his staff? Who knows where they would have ended up? They might still be circling the desert!

You see, God may be maturing you for a day yet to come. We usually don't want to hear those kinds of words. We want instant fulfillment. "I got a prophetic word and God said I'm going to do great things, so come on, God, let's get to it! It's time for me to do great things."

WE NEED TO UNDERSTAND THAT THE END GOAL OF OUR LIVES IS THE GLORIFICATION OF GOD, NOT THE FULFILLMENT OF OUR DESIRE.

I'm so glad that I don't always get my prayers answered the way I want them answered. If I had, the immature prayers that I prayed years ago would have yielded immature answers, answers that were probably more about my desires than about God's glory. We need to understand that the end goal of our lives is the glorification of God, not the fulfillment of our desire. Therefore I want nothing more than to walk out my life according to His will and His timeline, not mine. Sometimes our greatest promises are waiting for us at a much later date than we originally thought. One-week-old wine is never tasty. It needs the aging process. Sometimes, we do as well.

One of the most beloved pitchmen to ever appear on TV didn't arrive until after his retirement. His early life was nothing to be admired. He was a sixth-grade dropout, known for his temper as well as his failure. He worked hard to find jobs but had trouble keeping them. He was at one time or another a farmhand, a railroad worker, a fireman, a non-licensed lawyer (that one scares me), an insurance salesman, a gas station operator, an unsuccessful political candidate, and an amateur obstetrician (that one really scares me). All totaled, he was fired at least a dozen times.

Then, at the age of sixty-six, figuring he was done working, he took his Social Security check and decided to try one more time. This time he opened up a little chicken place where he sold chicken, cooked to his own rigid recommendations. His secret recipe became very popular and by 1970 there were over three thousand Kentucky Fried Chicken restaurants in over forty-eight countries. While most of the country was gearing up for retirement after sixty-five, Colonel Sanders was just beginning.

It's not too late! You're not too old! My sweet grandmother was a very religious person who attended church faithfully her whole life. Though she was a weekly church attendee, she had a revelation of Jesus as being her own personal Savoir when she was eighty-two years old. She lived another seventeen years, periodically having visions of Jesus' face smiling at her. One of her precious comments had to do with God giving her a chance to start over at eighty-two. I love that! Starting over at eighty-two. It's never too late!

Sometimes, because they've seen so much, those with added years (aka older folks) become more discouraged with life. They have seen a lot of people doing very foolish things during their years as a believer and often they hold on to pain and unforgiveness more easily than when they were younger. Whenever I feel myself headed in that direction I think back to David's precious wisdom from Psalm 37:25–26: *"I have been young and now I am old, yet I have not seen the righteous forsaken or his descendants begging bread. All day long he is gracious and lends, and his descendants are a blessing"* (NASB).

David did not allow the years to make him bitter, though he had plenty of reasons to do so. Instead of allowing his circumstances to dictate his heart, David continued to see God as continually being faithful and gracious and, in spite of others' shortcomings, he saw God's people as blessed. May we have his heart on such matters!

Hey, older folks, here's one more word of encouragement from David: *"The righteous man will flourish like the palm tree, he will grow like a cedar in Lebanon. Planted in the house of the LORD, they will flourish in the courts of our God. They will still yield fruit in old age…"* (Psalm 92:12–14).

*"They will still yield fruit **in old age**…."* Yes! I'm not dead yet. Till then, as long as there's breath, let's pray that the fruit of our older years continues to be even more bountiful and sweet.

ROOTED AND GROUNDED IN LOVE

For us in the real world, the thing that usually holds us back is not what's outwardly confronting us at the moment, but what we're inwardly battling. If we believe we're "too this" or "too that" we will often completely remove ourselves from the picture.

I know too many people who see themselves as lesser than they truly are. Their gifts may be amazing and wherever they go favor awaits them, yet they have such a small view of themselves and of the power of God inside them that they remain forever outside of what God has for them because of the inside battle.

I recently talked to one of the most gifted people I know, a brilliant artist and medical professional. After going to school to become a nurse practitioner, Mayo Clinic created a job in their surgical department just for her. That's what I call favor! She's in her mid-thirties and yet, during our conversation, she told me that she doesn't understand how anyone could, or should, allow her to be responsible for so many patients. She admitted that in her mind she often sees herself as still being a teenager.

I can relate. Not with the gifting and brilliant part, but with seeing myself as being younger. In some ways it can be healthy— if I see myself as a younger man, I will act and feel like a younger man. Okay, sounds good so far. But, if my view of myself as a younger man is actually that of a less mature, inexperienced, or even an unseasoned man, I will constantly be undercutting what God has been doing in my life for years.

For all those who see themselves as "lesser than" I have a challenge for you. Go to some of your closest friends and ask them this question: "What are three things you see in me that are positive and life-giving to you and to others?" We hear and feel too much negativity in our lives. Listen, I can't see the back of my head. I need another set of eyes to see that. We see only so much of ourselves. Let others tell you what God has already been trying to tell you. Again, even they only see so much of you but God sees the whole you and He thinks you're pretty amazing. So much so, He paid the greatest price to win you to His heart.

I had the privilege of working alongside an amazing man for over a decade. He was gifted in many areas, yet in spite of his many successes, he remained very humble. With success comes controversy and he had his share. But whether his press was good or bad, his gracious nature remained the same. One day I heard him say something that he had probably said a thousand times before, but for me, this first time I heard it, it immediately made its way into my heart: "Don't believe your press. You're not as great as others think you are, but you're not as bad as they think you are either."

That little phrase became a lifeline for me. When exuberant praise comes my way, I choose not to let it influence who I am. I know I'm not that amazing (down South they say, "you're not all that and a bag of chips"). Yet I know that when criticism arrives, I can sift out the truth and not give place to those things that are out to tear me down. I know that I'm loved by a God who loves me perfectly. That is my root system. When you are rooted and grounded in love, the winds of adversity can only affect you so much. They lose the power to control or devastate you. You are set free to be the man or woman God has called you to be, no matter your age or experience.

What are your "inner limits?" What limits have you placed upon yourself for whatever reasons, or what limits have you allowed others to place upon you?

Do you always see yourself as too young? Those who are stuck in a "too young" mentality are always deferring to those who are close to their age or older. They are so focused on their inexperience and their still-perceived youth that, as they age, they still see themselves as "the kid." As a result, their life is rarely about becoming a father or a mother. They just want to get what they need to survive well.

How about those who see the younger generation rising up and find themselves continually intimidated by them? For whatever reason, they can never seem to bridge the gap between themselves and those who are younger. The threat of youth is ever before them and as a result there is little trust or responsibility given to them. It's another spin on the old saying: "hurt people hurt people." Often, leaders who were hurt by leadership when they were young find it hard to release what they fought so hard to obtain. The answer to their freedom is forgiveness. It always is. None of us can change the past, but through forgiveness we can change the *effects* of the past. Maybe what we need is a new saying: "Healed people heal people."

So maybe you don't see yourself as too old or too young, but you have another "too" living inside you. What is it? Can you verbalize it? Are you too hurt? Too country? Too cultured? Too messy? Too angry? (For all of the above, see previous paragraph.)

Are you too inexperienced? If so, begin with something that will fill the needs of others rather than the need to fulfill your own desires. I have known gifted people who are waiting for something big to come their way and so they sit…waiting for their well-deserved invitation while they could be serving multitudes around them. Gain experience as a servant and you won't believe the doors that God will open for you.

Here's the bottom line. If we were not too sinful to be loved by God then there is nothing that is "too" anything for us. Too young to lead? Then serve! Too old to play? Then coach! Too hurt to help? Then heal by helping!

Good works have gotten a bad rap. It's absolutely true that we are saved by faith and not by our good works, no matter how great they may appear to the world. But, even though we are not saved by good works, we were saved *for* good works. Ephesians 2:10 says, *"For we are His workmanship, created in Christ Jesus for*

good works*, which God prepared beforehand that we would walk in them*" (NASB). God has prepared within us works or goodness and His desire is that we should walk in them.

Look at these other admonitions from the Word of God inviting us into a life of serving and displaying good works:

At Joppa there was a certain disciple named Tabitha, which is translated Dorcas. This woman was full of good works and charitable deeds....   (Acts 9:36)

Let them do good, that they be rich in good works, ready to give, willing to share....   (1 Timothy 6:18)

...in all things showing yourself to be a pattern of good works; in doctrine showing integrity, reverence, incorrupt-ibility.   (Titus 2:7)

...who gave Himself for us, that He might redeem us from every lawless deed and purify for Himself His own special people, zealous for good works.   (Titus 2:14)

The key to being set free from the prison of being "too" something is to find a place to serve others. Let your life testify of God's goodness through your own acts of love and kindness and people will soon see that you're not "too" anything. They will first see a selfless person, not a young person. They will see a zealous man or woman serving others, not an old man or woman.

As a worship leader, I've had people in my band as young as fourteen and as old as sixty-seven. I look for heart and so does God. Let others see your heart and they will soon stop seeing your perceived limitations.

Let me end with one more Scripture. This is our open door to a new life: *Let your light so shine before men, that they may see your good works and glorify your Father in heaven* (Matthew 5:16).

In the end, it's all about His glory, not mine and not yours. May our lives reveal His heart and purpose and leave people enjoying His fragrance.

6

CHARACTER-DRIVEN

I want to start out this chapter with two true stories. Each carries a great lesson by itself but together they form an eternal truth: character does matter.

STORY #1

Al Capone! Just his name conjures the worst of the worst. From 1925 until his imprisonment in 1932, Capone was the notorious gangster who ruled the Chicago mafia with an iron fist. He ensnared the Windy City in everything from bootlegged booze and prostitution to murder. He had no scruples about killing in cold blood when needed to keep his ring in control, and was responsible for the infamous St. Valentine's Day Massacre.

The man who successfully kept Capone out of prison for years was his lawyer, "Easy Eddie." He made the impossible look easy, hence his nickname. Time after time, Easy Eddie's legendary lawyerly skills kept Capone out of jail. Capone was always one to show his appreciation—that is, if you served him well, as Easy Eddie certainly did. To show his appreciation, Capone gave Easy Eddie a huge, beautiful fenced-in mansion. His property actually took up an entire city block…in downtown Chicago! With drivers, maids, and full-time assistants, Easy Eddie was in want of nothing.

Eddie had a soft spot, though, and that was his son. He knew that his ties to Capone would eventually affect his son's future, and he wanted better for his little boy. He could give his son everything he could ever want in terms of clothes, cars, and education, but he knew all that would not make up for a lack of character. Because of Eddie's lifestyle and behavior, carrying the family name would be a burden, not a gift, for his son.

So one day Eddie chose to do the unthinkable. He chose to do something that would speak of integrity to his son. After years of working for Capone, he left the mob in 1930 and chose to testify for the FBI in Capone's tax evasion trial. Largely because of Easy Eddie's testimony, Capone was finally put away in prison. Eddie knew that he had probably signed his own death warrant, but it was worth it for the effect it might have on his son. A few years later, at the age of forty-six, Easy Eddie was gunned down on his way home from work. No arrest was ever made, but everyone knew who had given the order.

When his body was found, the police removed a number of religious objects from his pockets along with a simple poem. The poem read:

The clock of life is wound but once,
And no man has the power

To tell just when the hands will stop,
At late or early hour.

The present only is our own.
Live, love, toil with a will.
Place no faith in time,
For the clock may soon be still.

STORY #2

A young American named Lieutenant Commander "Butch" O'Hare was assigned to the carrier *Lexington* in the South Pacific during World War II. On February 20, 1942, Butch and his entire squadron were sent on a mission. Shortly after becoming airborne, Butch noticed someone had forgotten to top off his fuel tank. If he continued on with the mission, he would not be able to return to the ship. He relayed the information to his flight leader and was instructed to turn around and head back to the Lexington. Reluctantly, he did.

On his flight back he noticed something that made his heart skip a beat. A squadron of Japanese bombers was headed toward his ship and the rest of the fleet. Knowing that all the American planes were on a sortie and he would not be able to get to them to return in time, Butch did the only thing he could think of. He headed right toward the Japanese squadron.

With 50-caliber guns firing at him from all sides, he continued on, firing at as many planes as he could. Even after his ammunition was spent, he continued on, trying to clip a plane's wing or tail. Finally, after five planes were destroyed, the Japanese squadron took off, and their planned attack was brought to an early end.

Butch O'Hare and his battered fighter barely made it back to the carrier.

The camera mounted on his plane showed the extent of his bravery, and he became the Navy's first WWII Ace and was awarded the Medal of Honor, the first Naval Aviator to receive this honor. A year later he was killed in a nighttime aerial attack, trying once again to save his ship. His hometown of Chicago wanted the world to remember his bravery and decided to rename its airport in his honor. We now know it as Chicago's O'Hare Airport.

LIFE OF INTEGRITY

Two stories that speak of bravery and integrity. So do they have anything more than that in common? I'm so glad you asked. Yes, of course they do. Butch O'Hare was "Easy Eddie's" son. They both carried the same name: Edward O'Hare.

Easy Eddie turned away from a life of deceit and corruption and embraced integrity, maybe for the first time in his existence. His choice reverberated through the country, finally landing in his son's lap. His son became a hero because he chose to embrace bravery, honor, and character. Thanks to Butch, men from many ships were able to go home to their loved ones. Easy Eddie may have lost his life, but the choice he made saved hundreds, if not thousands of lives.

Our word *integrity* comes from the Latin word, *integritatem*, which means "soundness or wholeness." Another meaning given that I particularly like is "uncorrupted virtue." Wow, uncorrupted virtues! Wouldn't that be nice to see in our world today? A person with integrity is one of life's greatest gifts. Unlike most gifts, though, it's a gift that right here, right now, we can choose to open and give to ourselves. When we do, we set ourselves up for the trust of family, friends, and even strangers, for open doors, and for opportunities that others will never see. That is the power of character and integrity.

The apostle Paul says in 1 Corinthians 9:24, *"Do you not know that those who run in a race all run, but one receives the prize? Run in such a way that you may obtain it."* Some take this as a type of Christian competition. "Come on, Chris, keep running hard and you'll end up closer to the throne when you get to heaven!" Others see it as a command to never slow down and never rest. Either option sounds dreadful to me. Paul's not asking us to race one another and try to beat those around you in some type of Christian Olympics. He's letting us know that *life brings reward if we choose wisely.*

Yes, good character and integrity are their own rewards, but when our lives express those traits, we win on every level.

Paul describes in Colossians what a life of integrity actually looks like. Colossians 3:12–13 reads:

Therefore, as the elect of God, holy and beloved, put on tender mercies, kindness, humility, meekness, longsuffering; bearing with one another, and forgiving one another, if anyone has a complaint against another; even as Christ forgave you, so you also must do.

Tenderness, humility, meekness, kindness...not words that you often associate with someone who "made it big" in their chosen field. But God's kingdom is not the kingdom of this world. In this world, some, like Al Capone, reach success through the most wretched lifestyle. Joseph Stalin reached the pinnacle of leadership of the Soviet Union, but if he had written a memoir it should have been titled, *How to Attain Power Through Every Kind of Evil Means Possible.* I enjoy history as much as the next person, but it doesn't always work well as a "how to." Instead, if we're walking with God, whether we "get ahead" or not, His nature and personality should be rubbing off on us and manifesting in tenderness, humility, meekness, and kindness. Especially since He has deposited His Spirit within us.

There are many positive character traits that bosses, coworkers, family members, and friends absolutely love and that can make all the difference in your life, your work, your church, and your home. I say "just a few" because the list goes on and on. Here's a baker's dozen.

Honesty

Adaptability

Authenticity

Kindness

Patience

Loyalty

Availability

Thoroughness

Friendly

Dependable

Generous

Courteous

Respectful

Notice that many of these are not accomplishments as much as they are manifestations of the state of our heart. Words like *kind, patient, friendly,* and *courteous* don't center on one's ability, they all speak to how one person treats another. Do you want your gifts to be unhindered? Then take note on how you treat those around you.

Who would you rather work with, someone friendly or someone who is always on the edge of anger? Who would you rather hire, a dependable, respectful person or a lazy, disloyal person? The answers are all too obvious. Like I said, *what we do* is eventually overshadowed by *who we are*.

Well, I guess when you make one list you need to make a contrary list. Or maybe I don't "need" to but I'm going to anyway. Here is a list I created (winnowed down from a much longer one) of negative traits that hinder growth, relationships, and opportunities for advancement:

Artificial

Cold

Disloyal

Impolite

Talks nonstop

Rude

Conceited

Bossy

Jealous

Crude

Angry

Two-faced

Lazy

That last list makes my stomach turn. Maybe yours does too, as you think of times you've been stuck in one trait or another— or watched a friend get stuck. I'm sure I've been guilty of each one of those negative traits during my life. Let's move on, then, to what our goal and heart's desire *should* be: to have the fruit of the Spirit as the hallmark of our lives. This is the greatest list. Galatians 5:22–23 says, "*...but the fruit of the Spirit is love,* *joy, peace, longsuffering, kindness, goodness, faithfulness, gentleness, self-control. Against such there is no law."*

"*Against such there is no law!*" That's one of my favorite sentences in the entire Word of God. It simply means that there is no restriction in the giving of these precious expressions. There is no place on earth where there is too much love or too much joy. It reminds me of an old Bee Gee's song called "Too Much Heaven." One of the lines goes, "Nobody gets too much love anymore. It's as high as a mountain and harder to climb." Can we have too much goodness or an over-abundance of kindness? Absolutely not! It's our invitation to not hold back in pouring out His nature and personality through our lives. That's called character!

GIFTS AREN'T ENOUGH

God loves to showcase Himself through us by giving us gifts and callings. Incredibly, our gifts and callings are irrevocable, or as the Easy-to-Read translation says, "*God never changes his mind about the people he calls. He never decides to take back the blessings he has given them*" (Romans 11:29 ERV). Amazing! God entrusts us with some of the most incredible gifts and talents, and when we choose to walk corruptly, He lets us continue on with our gifts intact. That said, though our gifts and calling may never be taken away from us, if we have no integrity and do not walk with a godly character, the opportunities to *use* our gifts and calling may be removed.

There are no excuses for a lack of character—no matter how gifted you are. What makes a company, an organization, or a church hire someone? Skills, yes. Experience, yes. But remember that the list of people with those skills and that experience is probably as long as your arm. Whatever the organization, they often want something more—they want to *trust* the new hire. Deciding to have strangers come in and become part of running "your baby" can be a daunting, even scary decision. That's why character is so important. Your gifts may open doors for you, but lack of character or integrity could send you right back out that same door.

I'm reminded of a man who was a rising star in his church world. He was charismatic, had a gift to teach, and was loved by all. Unfortunately, he had a hidden life that included inappropriate behavior with children. It was secret for many years but, as is often the case, what was hidden came to light. Now, this man's ministry gifts were real. He was and still is a gifted speaker. He was and still is a gifted singer. Unfortunately, he and his gifts are hidden away in prison for many years to come. They haven't been taken away, but thanks to his lack of character, they have lost the influence for which they were originally intended.

YOUR GIFTS MAY OPEN DOORS FOR YOU, BUT LACK OF CHARACTER OR INTEGRITY COULD SEND YOU RIGHT BACK OUT THAT SAME DOOR.

I have listened to people over the years complain about a job or a church leader that has not allowed them to walk out their calling. They might say things like, "They're holding me back and I don't know why." Or, "I don't understand why they're so controlling." Or the classic, "I could run this place better than they could any day." Sometimes it's true that poor leadership is creating frustration and heartache. Most often, though, it's the person's own unchecked or unaddressed character problems that are keeping them from getting ahead. Generally, people don't see those weak areas in their lives or they don't think those weak areas are important enough to hold them back. They're living in a prison they don't notice.

This book is about the holding patterns, the hindrances, the muddy puddles that get us stuck and keep us and our gifts from moving forward. One of, if not *the* most significant of these hindrances, is the simple truth of our own personality. And consequently, of the greatest gifts we can have is the ability to see ourselves as who we really are. Honestly acknowledging how we affect those around us, both positively and negatively, is a gift that brings great rewards.

I'm not in any way implying that we should believe the lies that the enemy of our soul speaks about us, telling us that we are unworthy for this or that. The lies he brings are meant to produce deception and destruction. Rather, I'm talking about our unique God-given personalities. Although we are loved, perfectly, by a perfect God, we unfortunately grow up in a very imperfect world that puts us through a gauntlet of experiences which produce areas of strength but also produce areas of weakness. Some people have gifts that are never seen because of their minefield of fragility, instability, and pain.

For example, you may have a gift of wisdom, but if you always seem to talk nonstop, your gift will soon find itself set to the side. The gift isn't invalid, but the package makes it very hard to receive what you have to say. A constant barrage of words gets very tiring to listen to. People can only hear so much at one time. Carrying on an actual conversation with someone like this is very difficult because it's nearly impossible to get a word in edgewise. Even when you do, your words are limited because the "talker" is waiting for something, anything, that can be turned back around for them to begin their next soliloquy. My heart aches for them. If they would only realize that the ability to bring restraint to their words would actually open the door for more of their input, release more of their gifting, and bring a greater purpose to their lives. Our influence is not in the abundance of our words, but in the abundance of His character within us.

Or you may have a gift of discernment, but if you are always meddling in other peoples' business, your gift has turned into an annoyance that could have serious consequences.

You may have a gift of administration, but if you are always scheduling and never relaxing, you may turn into a controlling person. Unable to live in the moment, you might become the last person someone looks to when they just need a shoulder to cry on or an afternoon spent doing nothing.

You may have a gift of creativity, but if you can't ever meet deadlines, you are actually hurting the people around you. Instead of looking to you for help on a project or idea, people will shy away from your gift because it's packaged up in procrastination.

NO EXCUSES

Remember, we aren't two people, one at work and one at home. All too often, gifted people are highlighted in public only to return home and have to deal with life as a "normal" person. For some, the switch is too much. They allow their public status to give them an exalted view of themselves until they think they are "above" normal life. I've seen great preachers turn into ogres in restaurants—they just waxed eloquent on the things of God at church only to act like an impatient narcissist when ordering food for lunch.

In 1919 the Chicago White Sox were accused of taking bribes to let the Cincinnati Reds win the World Series. A young boy purportedly said to one of the accused baseball players,

Shoeless Joe Jackson, as he stepped out of the courtroom, "Say it ain't so!" That story is more than likely a legend, but the cry of the disillusioned has been in my heart a number of times over the years—and maybe yours too. Another pastor, musician, writer, or leader, whose private life just doesn't line up with the public one. "Ah, come on, say it ain't so!" I love witnessing the gifts in action in amazing people, but let's never forget that what we do is eventually overshadowed by who we are.

One business article I read explained that business owners will test authenticity in interviewees by closely observing them during the short period of the first interview. Then, if that person returns for a second or third interview and they see the same person acting in the same manner, the business leader is much more likely to hire that person instead of someone with similar or higher qualifications. Authenticity and dependability are character traits greatly desired in any workplace.

Why is being authentic so difficult? Why is maintaining honesty so rare? Because it's not in our nature to be full of integrity. Paul says in 2 Corinthians 4:7, "*...we have this treasure in earthen vessels, that the excellence of the power may be of God and not of us.*"

Like it or not, we are simply earthen vessels. By ourselves, we are weak. Yet we are vessels that carry around the most precious thing known to man, the presence of God. How we carry His presence really matters. If I were to hand you a bucket filled with rubber balls, you wouldn't worry if one or two accidently fell out. But if I handed you an urn with the remains of your mother, you would hold it carefully, move very slowly, and make sure that it was always safely taken care of. How much more should we be circumspect, knowing that we are carrying about within us the very presence of God? We must be aware that how we carry Him determines how He manifests through us.

Jesus was pretty clear that for new wine to be fully used it needed to be put into new wine skins. In Mark 2:22, He says, *"And no one puts new wine into old wineskins; or else the new wine bursts the wineskins, the wine is spilled, and the wineskins are ruined. But new wine must be put into new wineskins."* We have to carry His life in a container that has been made new. Otherwise we leak!

Most people aren't aware that they leak. Obviously I'm not talking about dealing with some kind of physical condition. I'm talking about us as spiritual individuals and what's inside. We think that we are able to hide our areas of weakness from others, and for the most part, we do a fair job. We think that we're able to completely see our true self and express what's exactly needed at the moment. What we don't realize is that others have a 360-degree view of us. They may notice little things that we may never see. They also see our faces, which reveal more than we even realize. We can only see our faces when we're in front of the mirror. James warns against this very thing: *"But be doers of the word, and not hearers only, deceiving yourselves. For if anyone is a hearer of the word and not a doer, he is like a man observing his natural face in a mirror; for he observes himself, goes away, and immediately forgets what kind of man he was"* (James 1:22–24).

Are you prone to forget what kind of man or woman you are? Are you stuck in the mentality of blaming other people or circumstances for your situation, instead of your own decisions? Are you living in excuses instead of reasons? Reasons have purpose. Something does or doesn't happen for a reason. But excuses are created to cover something up. If I'm late for work, I can give a reason or I can give an excuse. The scenario might be as follows: I was watching a movie late into the night and the next morning I'm exhausted when the alarm rings. I hit "snooze" but I actually hit the "off" button and the next thing I know it's an hour later. The *excuse* is that my alarm didn't go off. The *reason* is that I was up too late, needed more sleep, and in the process, I mismanaged my alarm and overslept. A person of character finds the reason for his or her actions. A person without character simply finds an excuse for his or her actions.

Since we cannot control every action or circumstance that comes our way, we need to become people of action, not reaction. Godly character has built within it the ability to respond to adverse situations with the fruit of the Spirit. Without His character traits working within us, we become puppets to those things around us. They control us just as if we were tied with strings to the source of our trouble.

GODLY CHARACTER HAS BUILT WITHIN IT THE ABILITY TO RESPOND TO ADVERSE SITUATIONS WITH THE FRUIT OF THE SPIRIT. WITHOUT HIS CHARACTER TRAITS WORKING WITHIN US, WE BECOME PUPPETS TO THOSE THINGS AROUND US.

There's a big difference between reacting and responding. Reacting is commonly associated with some kind of quick reflex, usually not connected to wisdom, logic, or judgment. Something, or someone, pulls the strings and there we go— we're off to the races. On the other hand, when we respond, we are doing so from a place of what's been processed in our thoughts. It is the outpouring of our spirit and because of that, *we* pull the strings. We were not made to be people of reaction, but people of action.

Proverbs 2:20–21 reads, *"So you will walk in the way of the good and keep to the paths of the righteous. For the upright will inhabit the land, and those with integrity will remain in it..."* (ESV).

Walking in a godly manner allows us to inhabit lands that others never will, and it's those with integrity who will remain in that land. It's not a physical land; no, the one He longs to inhabit most is the garden of our heart. That is the land where He will remain.

I love this quote from Charles Swindoll's devotional *Day by Day*. It may sound a bit dated but its truth is eternal: "Few things are more infectious than a godly lifestyle. The people you rub shoulders with everyday need that kind of challenge. Not prudish. Not preachy. Just cracker-jack clean living. Just honest to goodness, bone-deep, non-hypocritical integrity."

Perfectly said! That's what we need, in our nation, in our communities and churches, and mostly within ourselves. If I'm going to leak anything, I want it to be His character, His nature, His wisdom, and His love. We are known by our gifts for only so long, then, after a period of time, our character takes center stage.

We started this chapter with two stories about two very different men who both acted bravely. But when we realized that these men were father and son, it gave us a more complete picture of the power of integrity. We need to remember that we are not living for ourselves. There are people watching and waiting to see men and women who really do walk in righteousness and deal with each other with integrity and godly character. The kids around us, whether in family or church, are bombarded with stories and images of character after character who display nothing even close to integrity. Often the hero is more of an anti-hero, someone who is just a bit less deranged than the villain. With those as the prevalent role models, we are even more responsible to walk in Christ's character and His nature. He's the source of all that's good.

I'll finish with this admonition, and yet promise, from Proverbs 20:7: *"The righteous who walks in his integrity—blessed are his children after him!"* (ESV). May the children of our generation see Him in our lives, and in so doing, may they live a happier and more fulfilled life because of the choices we've made.

7

THE POWERFUL REALITY OF DREAMING

On May 22, 1843, one thousand people gathered in Elm Grove, Missouri. They were nervous, yet filled with great excitement. They were doing something that people have been doing since the dawn of mankind, moving from one place to another. But this wasn't just any move down the street or to the next town. This was the day the first major wagon train would head out into what was becoming known as the Oregon Trail. There had been a number of missionaries and fur trappers who had lived in the Oregon Territory for years, but this was the first time such a large group would venture out together to travel for over two thousand miles with their families and life's goods piled high in a wagon.

Everything for them was a first. The wagons, which numbered more than one hundred, were not something most of these people had traveled in before. Most were farmers who rarely ventured far from their homes, yet they were traveling miles in the hopes of a better life. They discovered new dangers along the way, from river crossings to rampant diseases.

After much hardship and the loss of many lives, the vast majority of this first large contingent made it safely to their destination, the lush and fertile lands of western Oregon. The migration the following year was a bit smaller, but in 1845 nearly three thousand people made the trek across the country. After that time, the migration West became almost commonplace. Even though over time people knew more about what to expect, I'm sure it was not an easy thing. Then again, moving never is.

Now *pioneer* is used to describe anyone who is attempting to lead the way and be the first. Pioneering is difficult because there is no guide. There's no model and no framework from which to draw inspiration or courage. Even when you can see examples all around you of what you want to do or where you desire to go, stepping into something new is never easy. It's always easier to remain stuck than to do what is necessary to become unstuck.

Are you meant to be a pioneer? What seems to be tugging at your heart lately? Is there something that God has given you that burns within you? Something new that seems impossible?

BORN CREATIVE

"In the beginning God created..." (Genesis 1:1). We have a God who from the first words of Scripture is described as a Creator. That's what He did because that is who He is. Then He turns around and creates us in His own image. The urge churning within us to make, do, or change, is a direct result of how we were made. We have within our very nature the God-given gift to create! Now, we can't create something from nothing like He did, but we can use our gift of creativity to expand,

enlighten, and beautify our world, not just for ourselves, but for others as well.

Creativity is one of God's greatest gifts. To write words that have never been written and have them move the heart is priceless. To witness an artist paint a picture of what before they had only seen in their mind is mind-boggling to me. Or when I gaze at a magnificent sculpture—*wow!* For someone to see a beautiful image hidden within a block of granite is one thing. For them to then create something extraordinary from it by removing everything around it—that astounds me.

I believe everyone has the ability to create beauty. That's God's nature and we're made in His image. Now, that doesn't mean we can all draw like Leonardo da Vinci. I just wanted to draw like my older sister, but I couldn't even do that. My drawings always looked like rejects from a bad cartoon. I remember my junior high art teacher asking me why I always drew a jet airplane. "It's the only thing I can draw that actually looks like what I'm drawing," I answered. She asked me to try other things, which I did, but eventually, even she agreed with me. She said, "Well, Chris, at least you can draw a decent-looking jet." To this day, I can still draw that jet. Further proof that God doesn't remove our gifts from us. If you ever need a picture of a 1960s military jet, just let me know.

So sports became my go-to creative expression and for years I gave myself to each and every sport I could. But after an ankle injury in high school ended my sports dreams, I began to wonder if I had anything else going for me or if I was I going to become what I always dreaded—someone who had a few good years in high school and didn't have anything else going for him after that.

During my time recuperating from my ankle injury, my father bought me a cheap guitar so I would have something more to do than watch TV. As I began to play and hear the notes and chords, I suddenly realized that melody lines were flowing through my head. Each new chord or rhythm brought new melody lines. So much so that some nights I could barely get to sleep because I was playing them over and over in my mind. Little did I know then that music would become one of the primary callings of my life and that creating new music would be a big part of that calling. Today, I am still creating new songs because I still hear those melody lines. May they never stop! Well, maybe when I really need to get to sleep.

I've been a believer and a follower of Jesus since August of 1973. Since that time I have heard some amazing (and not so amazing) music come out of the church. I've loved every stage, from Maranatha's simple, yet beautiful, worship albums in the '70s to worship taking off with Hosanna, Integrity and then Vineyard Music. Each one brought a new form of worship expression to the church. But the one that had the newest sound and greatest impact on me was from a church in England. Their initial cassette tapes were titled *Cutting Edge*, and believe me, they were. Martin Smith and *Delirious?* brought forth a totally new sound. Many people say that they ushered in the modern worship movement. Their writing was intended not just to capture a tune but to capture a generation for Jesus, and they did. A friend returned from England in 1994 and handed me two cassette tapes. When I put them on it reminded me of the moment I first heard the Beatles. It was new, it was fresh, but more than that, it had something different. With songs like "I Could Sing of Your Love Forever," "History Maker," "My Glorious," "Did You Feel the Mountains Tremble?", "Shout to the North," "Deeper," "Majesty (Here I Am)," and "What a Friend I've Found," worship became something more than an expression of one heart. More than even the sound of a church. Worship now had a universal sound. It was now the sound of *the* church.

God didn't just create something new in the garden. In Isaiah 43:19, He said, *"For I am about to do something new. See, I have already begun!"* (NLT). He didn't stop in the garden and He didn't stop in Isaiah. Second Corinthians 5:17 declares, *"Therefore, if anyone is in Christ, he is a new creation. The old has passed away; behold, the new has come"* (ESV). God is still doing a new thing. Creating new lives within people so that those new people can create according to what He placed in them. But although creation is effortless for God, for us it can have some major obstacles.

STUCK IN THE DREAM

I wrote a song shortly after I moved to Nashville, Tennessee, about being a dreamer. After meeting person after person who had moved there to pursue their dream of making it in the music business, it soon became apparent that not all of them would achieve their dream. Some would, some would come up just short, some would leave and find their life's call elsewhere, and some would find themselves working in the music business, just not as a singer/songwriter. But no matter where they landed, I wanted to address the dreamer within us all and encourage people to not give up so easily. The second verse and the chorus to my song go like this:

Dreamers are a funny lot—misunderstood by most.
Always looking for some future day.
But that's the only way to look—when you have a dream.
Otherwise your dream just fades away.

Just don't let those whose dreams have died, steal yours away.
Hold on till the river meets the sea
Hold on till the winter becomes spring
Hold on to your dreams—Hold on.

Moving ahead with your dream or goal requires some clear-cut strategies. Three absolutes are always before us in order to accomplish what's in our heart. Those three are *time, energy,* and *resources.* Every new endeavor to actualize our dreams takes all three. (Of course, in our day, *resources* usually means *money.*) The alternative is to remain right where you are. Now, if right where you are is a great place, praise God! Rejoice and be grateful for the season you're in. But if this is the tenth season of the same pressure-filled, life-straining season, it may be time to say goodbye to where you are and start acting on your dreams. It may be time to actually start valuing what you say you value. If what you value never gets your time, energy, or money, it's not a real value. It's what I call a *desired* value. I've heard musicians say that they value excellence, but when I see their old cheap guitar that has no ability to stay in tune, I realize that they value the *idea* of excellence, but in reality, they are afraid to give up some personal money to actually obtain excellence. If weekly piano lessons are too expensive at $35.00 but we buy two $4.50 lattes a day, we say we value improving, but in reality we don't. We *want* to be better musicians, but we *value* lattes. The same is true for time and energy. Each one of these things is an indicator of what we really value as opposed to what we say we value.

Picture if you can, two rooms divided by a screen. You are in one room but your dream, your very heart's desire, yeah, that which you value the most, is in the other room. You can see it! You can almost touch it! The only thing standing in your way is a screen. It's not a thin screen, but something that almost looks like a barrier. Some people hit that screen and apply some energy, but after a little while they tire and then eventually come to the conclusion that it's really not worth it to expend all that energy, especially if they don't know whether they'll actually get what they're wanting. Slowly and quietly, they turn away and chase another dream, sometimes a lesser dream. Some people hit that screen for a few minutes, but after a little while they feel like they are wasting time, and they figure their time is better spent on something they *know* they can achieve. Quickly, so as to not waste time, they turn away and chase another dream. Some people come at the screen, realize right away that they need new equipment to get through the barrier, but don't want to spend any money. *If it's not free, it's not worth it,* they think, and turn away.

If it takes too much time...gone. Too much energy spent... gone. Too much money...gone. The problem for many today is that we expect the fulfillment of our dreams to come just as easily as posting our latest picture on Facebook. What this actually tells us is the level of value we place on our dreams. Those things that we highly value will grace us to let time, energy, and money be spent from our lives. It takes time and money to get a degree but if we have no value for that, we'll never take the time nor spend the money. It takes time and energy to run a marathon, but if we have no value for running a marathon we will never put in the time or energy to accomplish that goal. For anything of great value, it usually takes all three things to accomplish what we're after.

> **THE PROBLEM FOR MANY TODAY IS THAT WE EXPECT THE FULFILLMENT OF OUR DREAMS TO COME JUST AS EASILY AS POSTING OUR LATEST PICTURE ON FACEBOOK.**

A good understanding of time, energy, and money can help us know what truly burns in us or what we think we'd like. I know so many people who see something and say, "Oh, man, that's what I really want to do," when, in reality, they don't have any idea what it would take to achieve nor do they understand what it would mean to daily life if they did attain it.

When the realization of our desired value takes more than what we thought to accomplish so we set it aside, that's not necessarily wrong. There are things that I thought I longed for and wanted in the past, but when I began the process to attain them, I learned that what I was after wasn't actually what I originally thought.

My point, however, is that we should never, ever think that because something didn't come easily, it must not be worth it. Promises from God are often presented in the form of a struggle. Hebrews 12:2 reminds us, "*for the joy that was set before Him* [Jesus] *endured the cross….*" We, too, like Christ, are often called to *endure*. And the endurance often involves change.

CAUTION: DREAMING MEANS CHANGE

Change is never easy. As they say, the one thing in life that you can always count on is change. "New beginnings" sounds so romantic. "Starting out on a new adventure" conjures up the image of an old and loved fairy tale. It's good to remember, though, that every fairy tale comes with some kind of adversary, an enemy who waits for the right moment to strike in order to bring an end to the hero's or heroine's dreams. It's good to be prepared for whatever comes your way, not just practically, but with your heart set to, as my song says, "hold on till the winter becomes spring." In other words, we must be ready to endure!

When I was a little guy, my parents were going through marital and financial difficulties. Life was anything but stable. By the time I was eight years old, I had moved almost ten times. I remember that after one of the moves—I think I was four or five—I didn't even unpack my clothes. *Why bother?* I thought. I kept them in their big boxes and just hung them on the side of the box when they were dirty. As an adult, I've had to go back to address some of the negative side effects and issues from that time, but I do have at least one positive take-away from it. I didn't realize it at the time, but with each new move, I was learning how to adjust positively to change. I had to. Each new address brought new challenges that I had to either fight or embrace.

I applaud those who follow their dreams, but it's good to be aware that our dreams may change and morph into something else over time and we need to be okay with that. So many people have such great dreams, but moving from being a dreamer to a doer, from dreaming to reality, can be an incredible challenge, especially when you're venturing into the unknown. Sometimes it will mean moving into something that's new for you, which is difficult enough. But sometimes it will mean moving into something *no one* has ever done before, which is an even a greater challenge. However, there's a famous quote from an unknown writer that says it well: "Never be afraid to try something new. Remember, amateurs built the ark; professionals built the *Titanic*."

Think about what Noah must have gone through. No one had ever built a boat like the one God told Noah to build. I'm sure at the time there were boats for fishing or for transportation up and down rivers, but when God spoke about a boat that would be 450 feet x 75 feet x 45 feet, I'm sure Noah couldn't fathom what it would take to build something that huge. He had a goal in his heart and he knew what it would take to get there. Noah expended the time, the energy, and the resources in order to accomplish his dream of building the ark. He probably just never quite realized that it would take decades to build. I guess sometimes it's good not to know everything before we start something.

Genesis 12:1–4 says,

> *Now the* LORD *had said to Abram: "Get out of your coun-*
> *try, from your family and from your father's house, to a land*
> *that I will show you. I will make you a great nation; I will*
> *bless you and make your name great; and you shall be a*
> *blessing. I will bless those who bless you, and I will curse him*
> *who curses you; and in you all the families of the earth shall*
> *be blessed." So Abram departed as the* LORD *had spoken*
> *to him.*

Wow! What a promise! Talk about a new adventure! Let's read that again: *"I will make you a great nation; I will bless you and make your name great; and you shall be a blessing."* Yeah! Let's go out and be a great blessing! But what we often skip over is that there will be curses coming at us. He will curse those who curse us—but that means a curse will be coming our way. And when I say *curse*, I'm talking about opposition and pushback. In the midst of one of God's greatest promises, He makes it clear both that there will be opposition and that He will be with us through it.

KNOW THAT WHAT AWAITS YOU IN THE UNKNOWN IS THE FULFILLMENT OF FAITHFULNESS.

Knowing exactly where you'll be and what you'll be doing in the next five, ten, or twenty years might be a nice thing, but in all honesty, moving into the future, not fully knowing what the result will be, and going for it anyway, is and always will be a part of the Christian life. But it should always be a noble thing. There is excitement in the journey. Know that what awaits you in the unknown is the fulfillment of faithfulness. If we knew every-thing that would happen next in our lives, we would more than likely be miserable. What makes our lives exciting, challenging, and, in all honesty, even the least bit interesting, is living a life of faith, believing when we don't fully understand, and stepping out when things before us aren't fully clear.

My wife and I have made a number of moves during our life together. It's never been easy. Each move has been painful in one way or another. Some moves have taken us away from lifelong friends while others have taken us away from family. Yet each move has also added something wonderful to our lives. Wonderful things that never would have happened if we had stayed where we were. That's not a call to move around all the ime, but it is a reminder that when God calls us into something new, He will always be there with us.

C. S. Lewis once wrote to Mary Shelburne, an old frail woman nearing the end of her life: "There are better things ahead than any we leave behind."[6] He was trying to encourage her that no matter how wonderful this life had been, even better things awaited her in the life to come. I think we can also apply these words to this life. There are better things ahead. We may not fully see or know what those things are, but if we know His heart we can rest assured that there are truly better things ahead.

KNOW A GOOD THING WHEN YOU SEE IT

On the other side of the coin, seeing something new coming your way, knowing it will be a hit, and investing in it is not an easy thing to see. In July 1957, no one could have seen it coming. A young boy, age sixteen, asked his new friend, first name James, a fifteen-year-old, to join his band. In February of 1958 they ask James' younger friend, then age fourteen, to join the band as well. The band added and subtracted a couple of more

---

6. C. S. Lewis, *Letters to an American Lady* (Grand Rapids, MI: Eerdmans, 1967), 124.

people until August of 1962 when they finally asked Richard to be their drummer. The band was now complete.

When they went in to Decca records in January of 1962 to see if Decca was interested in producing them, Dick Rowe, Decca's main record executive and producer, had no idea that the decision he was soon to make would follow him for the rest of his life. After listening to their audition, he politely, but firmly, told them, "…guitar groups are on the way out" and added that the group "has no future in show business."

You know the group as the Beatles. John Lennon, (James) Paul McCartney, George Harrison, and Richard Starkey (aka Ringo Starr) seemed to come out of nowhere. Bebop music was in, as well as early rock and roll, and of course the popular music of the day (Frank Sinatra, etc.) was still being played. But if you were around at that time, and you heard "I Want to Hold Your Hand" or "She Loves You," you knew that you were hearing something new.

Imagine how Decca Records felt just a couple of short years later. To be honest, though, I don't blame them. We might think we would have signed the Beatles on the spot, but only hindsight is 20/20. It isn't easy knowing what sound, look, or trend is going to be the next big thing.

Similarly, we need to understand that we often have these God-desires within us, and that it will take initiative in any kind of planning stage as well as great intentionality on your part to achieve those goals.

THE ROLE OF A FRIEND

What will you pioneer? What is your gifting? You probably both know and don't know. What I mean is that most people have some idea of what they do well, but most people have not given themselves to their gifting in a way that would in fact show them the extent of what God has put within them. Not only that, we often only see a part of who we are, and therefore, only a part of what we're capable of doing. How many times have people been encouraged to do something that they themselves didn't see as a personal gift or a talent?

One of the most successful actors of our generation almost didn't become one. He had been in a few movies in the early '70s, but had never made a name for himself. Knowing that he was an excellent craftsman, he went back to work as a set carpenter and began to do well, enjoying his simple yet rewarding life. Something still burned within him to act, but there were no good opportunities. He knew he could have a steady job working with his much-beloved tools as opposed to pursuing the up-and-down world of acting.

Fortunately for him, he had a friend who saw something more in him. A casting consultant named Fred Roos told him that he would be perfect for a new film. Despite all the obstacles, Roos was unwavering in his belief that his friend would be perfect for one of the main roles—so much so that he arranged for his carpenter friend to be hired to install a door at the studio. When he got there, it wasn't long before the director began to see his potential, too. So Harrison Ford hung up his full-time carpentry job and took the role of Hans Solo in George Lucas's new movie, *Star Wars*.

Often, what we see as possibility within ourselves is seen by others as greatness. That's why it's always good to have people around you who can honestly speak into your life and give you their thoughts.

I realize that going after something new or seeing something new may not be an easy thing, but if we "Hold On," we may see not only the fulfillment of our hopes and dreams, but we may actually open the door for others to follow in our footsteps and go after their own heart's desires. Reasonable people walk through the world around them. Dreamers create the world around them.

But don't just be a dreamer. Act on those dreams.

I love this Seth Godin quote from his book *Tribes*. It simply says: "Paint a picture of the future. Go there; people will follow."

That's my call to myself and to you. Let's paint.

8

THE VOICE IN YOUR HEAD

Mike Krzyzewski and Phil Jackson are two of the most successful basketball coaches who've ever lived. Krzyzewski's success is in the college game while Jackson's is in the pros. As of this writing, Krzyzewski has won over 1,040 games as a coach, more than any other coach in NCAA history. Phil Jackson has won eleven NBA championships as a coach as well as two while he was a player for the New York Knicks.

However, though each man is looked up to and respected for their coaching skills, they are known for more than the number of their wins and looked up to for more than their sports skills. Both men have a history of not just coaching the game of basketball, but of coaching the characters of the young men who play.

It's so important to have people in our lives who do more than instruct. As it says in 1 Corinthians 4:15, *"For though you might have ten thousand instructors in Christ, yet you do not have many fathers...."* We need fathers and mothers, people who can steer sons and daughters with wisdom and grace.

Interestingly, from an early age, both Krzyzewski and Jackson were themselves mentored and influenced by their parents' life lessons. Mike Krzyzewski's mother made a point of saying to him when he was a young man, "Make sure you only let good people on your bus." This was her way of telling him to make sure that he surrounded himself with not just gifted people, but good people, people with integrity who will help in his journey of life to take him somewhere great.

Phil Jackson's father, a preacher and a man of great influence, used to have a plaque on his desk that young Phil would see whenever he entered. It read: "The bigger your head gets, the easier your shoes are to fill."[7] This plaque, as well as the man who owned it, had a tremendous impact on Phil's life. They both helped to shape not just the way he would someday coach, but also his thoughts about how integrity of character is more important that gifting. Later, basketball greats Michael Jordan, Shaquille O'Neal, and Kobe Bryant would each go on to say that Phil Jackson's voice echoed through their thoughts not just on the court but off it as well.

THE INFLUENCE OF OTHERS

Both Krzyzewski and Jackson knew what had influenced their lives, and this allowed them to influence others. *Influence*, what a powerful word! Its dictionary definition says it well: "the capacity or power of persons or things to

7. See Mike Sager, "Phil Jackson: What I've Learned," *Esquire*, May 8, 2011, http://www.esquire.com/sports/interviews/a4112/phil-jackson-0208/ (accessed May 15, 2017).

be a compelling force on or produce effects on the actions, behavior, opinions, etc., of others." A compelling force! Wow, that's huge! It's also what most of us desire to be. We want to be that someone who is able to affect the behavior, opinions, and even beliefs of others, and hopefully do it in a positive way. I'm sure if we stop for a moment and think, each of us can identify one or more people in our lives who have been that compelling force in helping to determine our own individual behavior.

THE INFLUENCE WE ALLOW TO ENTER OUR LIVES CAN LEAD US TO FULFILL OUR CALL AND DESTINY OR CAN DERAIL US FROM IT.

The influence we allow to enter our lives can lead us to fulfill our call and destiny or can derail us from it. I know too many people over the years who have slowly been turned away from walking with God under the influence of subtle words of doubt that replaced God's direction with another voice.

Does that sound like someone you know?

Does that sound like you?

Who you allow on your bus will determine where your bus ends up. Someone close to us can have so much influence over us that we find ourselves doing things we would have never dreamed of doing previously. This can be tremendously positive or it can prove to be very destructive. All too often the people we let on our bus take control of the driver's seat and steer it in directions we never wanted to go. In the right hands, influence is one of life's most wonderful gifts. In the wrong hands, it can be one of life's greatest terrors.

When I was in high school, I had two close friends. We were called the Triumvirate by a few of our friends—*triumvirate* being a word used to describe a close-knit group of three leaders. And leaders we all were. Whether leading in sports, in academics, socially, or in just plain foolishness, we were usually at the front of the line.

It was during this time that I found myself constantly being pulled in opposing directions. One of us would want to do something and before you know it, one or both of the others would be onboard, even if we didn't really want to be. One minute I'm acting wise beyond my years and the next minute I'm acting like a ten-year old. I was like a ship tossed to and fro, being moved about by the activity of the waves around me. At that time I didn't have 1 Corinthians 15:33 in my daily heart repertoire, but I wish I had: *"Do not be deceived: 'Evil company corrupts good habits.'"* Now, my friends weren't *evil*, but the meaning behind this verse still applies. Good habits can be corrupted by close relationships with ungodly people or people who still have a way to go toward maturity.

We have all grown up understanding the power of peer pressure, but what we might not realize is that so many of our past voices still occupy space in our brains, their old and tired whispers still finding a home in our thoughts. Peer pressure doesn't end with our teenage years. It's a powerful force that, if we let it, can continue to be a major influence in our lives. Again, not all peer pressure is bad. In fact, we have probably had more positive peer influences over the years than negative. That said, sometimes giving in to that one negative influence can have greater impact on your future than the dozen positive choices you previously made. Thank God for Romans 8:28, which assures us that *"all things work together for good to those who love God, to those who are the called according to His purpose."* He takes our worst decisions and somehow manages to create greatness. God is so very good.

I think it's true for most of us that we often do something (or don't do something) because of the opinions of others. I know that as I grew up, I could hear my mother say, "Don't run with scissors in your hands." I'm sure we can all hear our mothers say that. Or how about, "If you keep crossing your eyes, they will eventually stay that way." It turned out not to be true but, nonetheless, it sure had an effect on me. Those are pretty normal "mother sayings." Thankfully, most of us survived childhood with two eyes that weren't permanently crossed, all without being impaled by a pair of scissors. Thanks, Mom!

But then there are the voices in our heads that speak to us about the deeper, more meaningful things of life. Think of how easily people are influenced by celebrities—seen in the clothes they wear, the music they listen to, and even the body type they discipline themselves to have. Many of these supposed role models barely have their lives together and seem more focused on appearance than on anything else. And yet, here we are, as a culture, hanging on to their every thought and action.

In the late 1930s, the "celebrity" politician Winston Churchill influenced an entire nation to fight against an evil power—the Third Reich. Much can be learned from his strong communication skills, his innovation, and his trustworthiness, which made him one of the greatest leaders in history. A true inspiration, his principles are as relevant today in our uncertain climate as they were more than sixty years ago. His words instilled courage and strength into the nation of England when many other voices of his day were spewing fear and defeat. A great orator, his words became the thoughts of England, thoughts that helped win the crucial Battle of Britain as well as WWII. In preparation for that battle, Churchill spoke these words in a now-famous speech that *influenced* the entire world.

> We shall not flag or fail. We shall go on to the end, we shall fight in France, we shall fight on the seas and oceans, we shall fight with growing confidence and growing strength in the air, we shall defend our Island, whatever the cost may be, we shall fight on the beaches, we shall fight on the landing grounds, we shall fight in the fields and in the streets, we shall fight in the hills; we shall never surrender.[8]

This speech is famous not just for its brilliant style and elegance, but because it became the war cry for an entire nation.

If we could only understand the power of a single voice. Some, like Winston Churchill, had the power to galvanize an entire nation, giving them purpose and hope in the middle of great turbulence and turmoil. Unfortunately, at other times, one singular voice can lodge in our brains, bringing suspicion, vacillation, and potential heartache.

THE VOICE OF GOD

When I was in high school I was known as a very good athlete, especially at my favorite, track and field. A cousin of mine who had been in my high school and graduated a few years before I did once heard about a record jump that I had done. His first response was not to congratulate me but to instead simply say, "Well, that was a lucky jump. You'll never jump that far again, that's for sure." I did jump further, but it was a couple of practice jumps for the upcoming NYS Class C Finals. My first jump was another record-breaking jump but wasn't allowed

---

8. Winston Churchill, "We Shall Fight on the Beaches," WinstonChurchill.org, https://www.winstonchurchill.org/resources/speeches/1940-the-finest-hour/we-shall-fight-on-the-beaches (accessed June 2, 2017).

as it was a practice jump. My second practice jump was even further, but unfortunately no one thought a high school kid would jump that far so no one raked the very back of the pit. I landed directly on a rock that twisted my ankle, ripping it apart. Instantly my jumping days were over. My cousin was right: I never jumped that far in competition again.

Unfortunately, from that time forward his voice lingered in my mind. Every time something good would come my way or I began to move ahead in life, his voice would return and say, "That was just dumb luck. Don't get too excited, things won't turn out like you think they will."

It had happened while I was a junior in *high school* and yet for years his voice still had power in my life. I didn't initially attribute it to him as the incident had been long forgotten, but one day I recognized the connection to his voice (I actually heard his voice in my head) and focused my attention on removing it from my life forever. I loved my cousin then and I do to this day, but thankfully his voice of failure no longer exists in my head.

In a perfect world, we would never be affected by these voices, and instead always be led by the voice of God. That's the main voice that should be in our head, whispering wisdom and grace. As Jesus said in John 10:27, *"My sheep hear My voice, and I know them, and they follow Me."* Such a wonderfully true and accurate statement. He is our Good Shepherd and we are His sheep. We do hear His voice, and when we do, it's a joy to follow Him.

Unfortunately, for many of us, His voice is mixed in with other voices locked in our head from days long gone by, and I know for myself, not too infrequently it gets a little crowded in there. It reminds me of a time recently when I was watching a game on TV and two of my grandkids began to ask me questions, each one standing in a different corner of the room.

I diverted my attention away from the game but between their questions coming from two different places (literally and figuratively) and my still unwitting connection to the game, I found it nearly impossible to give any of the voices I heard the attention they deserved. I had to mute the TV and then take my granddaughters' questions one at a time. I had to remove all the distractions around me and intentionally focus. A true necessity in today's fast-paced digital world.

It's like that with God's voice. He always speaks clearly and with great love, but if our minds and thoughts are jumbled with multiple voices it can often be difficult to differentiate between one voice and another. *That's when we need to look into our own background and try to figure out whose voice has the most weight in our lives.* Was it a godly parent or was it a jealous, competitive friend? Was it a pastor who had our best interests in mind or was it someone who wanted to use us for their own gain?

GOD'S DESIRE IS THAT WE WOULD NOT JUST BE ABLE TO HEAR HIM FOR THE BIG DECISIONS IN OUR LIVES, BUT THAT WE WOULD HAVE A DAILY LIFE OF COMMUNION WITH HIM.

Many people I know still battle with voices from people in their past who called them "worthless," "ugly," "stupid," or "good-for-nothing." It may be true that sticks and stones can break our bones but it's not true that words can never harm us. Words can set you off in a direction that the Maker of Life never intended for you. But, we can change that because the One who writes our story is not yet done. He can bring in His heavenly eraser and erase what someone else tried to write on your heart. Only His words are eternal. Everything else is temporary and has only the power we allow it to have. He is not just the deliverer of our sins, He delivers us from the power of others who may have wittingly, or unwittingly, sinned against us.

If we're smart we'll recognize that the greatest voice to speak to us is God's voice, and that His Word is His voice. When we do that, we can fill ourselves up with His Word and we'll hear His voice all through the day.

God's desire is that we would not just be able to hear Him for the big decisions in our lives, but that we would have a daily life of communion with him. As it says in Isaiah 30:30, *"The LORD will cause His glorious voice to be heard."* How wonderful is that! He wants to make His voice heard.

We all know that following His voice is the wisest way to navigate through life but just as a reminder, here are a few verses to back that up:

In your seed all the nations of the earth shall be blessed, because you have obeyed My voice.   (Genesis 22:18)

Now therefore, if you will indeed obey My voice and keep My covenant, then you shall be a special treasure to Me above all people.   (Exodus 19:5)

But if you indeed obey His voice and do all that I speak, then I will be an enemy to your enemies and an adversary to your adversaries.   (Exodus 23:22)

And all these blessings shall come upon you and overtake you, because you obey the **voice** *of the LORD your God.*
      (Deuteronomy 28:2)

The common thread between these verses is that *a **voice brings with it a choice***. Every voice we listen to brings with it another potential choice. I don't think anyone reading this would disagree with me in saying that His voice should be the most prominent voice in our lives. When we hear His voice clearly we become confident in our direction. When it's mixed with other voices or when another voice has more weight than His, we find ourselves "obeying" that other voice. Oh, they might sound something like His voice, but often they are attached to past hurts or to people who once had a negative impact on your life. I would assume that if we are in a healthy community of God-lovers, that most of the voices around us echo His thoughts and speak with His heart, yet even there we need to make sure we have a good grasp on His Word so that He becomes our greatest sounding board.

STOP AND LISTEN

I can't jump through the pages of this book and stop your reading at this moment, but if I could, I would ask you these questions:

Who speaks to you internally?

Who influences you the most?

What voice has the most weight in your life and in your decisions?

Your honest answer can help free you in more ways than you can imagine.

Stop and listen…do your father's wise words still echo in your head, or do you hear his voice of shame? Did mom want a girl and when you, a boy, arrived, did you grow up hearing disdain in her voice? Do the mocking jeers of old schoolmates still have a place in your thoughts? Were you told that you would never be a success?

I was once told by a very loving mother figure in my life that, because of the path I took to follow the Lord, I would never make much money. I remembered right after that to wrap her state-ment in what God says about me and let it drift away. Will I ever make much money? I don't know, but I know this: if I don't, it won't be because someone's words had a negative effect on my thinking, and therefore my life. On top of that, I am very content with where God has me personally, relationally, physically, and financially. Because He's the author and the finisher of my faith and my life, I'll leave the rest to Him. (See Hebrews 12:2.)

Once you begin to rid the extemporaneous voices from your mind, it leaves you with a new strength to actually be a positive voice in the lives of others. I had the opportunity (and the joy) of teaching junior high for seven years. It was a wonderful season where I not only taught, but fathered. In all honesty, I learned just as much or more than my students. My greatest joy was not just watching them connect with what I was teaching, but watching them respond to my role as a father and a teacher of the heart. Through it, I learned just how much the junior high years are an impressionable time of life. To be able to speak des-tiny and purpose into their lives, as well as, hopefully, showcas-ing kindness and a desire for more of God, was one of the great-est privileges I have ever had. To have many of them come back to me over the years with testimonies of my impact on their lives is the icing on the cake.

The season of my life as a teacher was the time that an understanding of influence really came into focus for me. Before then, I was on a path of growth as a man, a husband, a father, and a child of God. That may sound great, but in all reality, I had never fully attached great meaning behind that growth. I wanted to grow in order to do something *great*, not in order to become a better person. But after teaching those kids, a major shift happened inside me. I saw that my growth and maturity was not just about me, it was also about those who would come into my sphere of influence each and every day. I felt for the first time an earnest hope and desire to impact the kids around me for the good. I was no longer just living for my world, I was now made for His pleasure and His purpose.

Coco Chanel, the French fashion designer and the name behind the Chanel brand, once said, "Success is often achieved by those who don't know that failure is inevitable." If we don't hear the voices of failure, maybe, just maybe, our thoughts will begin to turn toward thoughts of success.

I love Jesus' words from the gospel of John. After describing the plans of those who seek to be our enemies, He then describes His plan for our lives: *"I have come that* [you] *may have life, and that* [you] *may have it more abundantly"* (John 10:10).

What a voice to listen to! He came to give us life, and not just any kind of life, *abundant* life. That's the voice I want to hear in my head and that's the voice I want to convey to those around me. I love to listen to Him speak. Again, He says in Matthew 19:26, *"With men this is impossible, but with God all things are possible."* He is speaking truth to our future and our souls but also to our minds.

Here's one last quote from Winston Churchill. "You will never reach your destination if you stop and throw stones at every dog that barks." This is obviously addressing those who try to stop you and discourage you along the way, but it also speaks to the barking that past voices may have in our heads. If we listen to them we will forever be hindered in reaching our destination.

If Winston gets one more quote, than God surely gets to have one more. One more voice to encourage our hearts. From Revelation 21:3, a loud voice from heaven declares: *"Behold, the tabernacle of God is with men, and He will dwell with them, and they shall be His people. God Himself will be with them and be their God."*

That's our promise, right from His voice!

NOT ALL SHADOWS ARE BAD

At seventeen, at young man answered an advertisement in a local paper. Liberty Records was looking for new songwriters. It was the mid-sixties, the Beatles were changing the music scene all over the world, and this kid thought, *why not, maybe, just maybe, something will happen*. It had to be better than the rundown farm his father had recently bought where he spent hours working the land.

He was not selected for his songwriting, but somebody inside Liberty Records handed his lyrics over to a musician, also not selected, named Reginald Dwight. This man thought they could make a good writing duo. He was right. So began a friendship and a partnership that, as of this writing, has accumulated multiple Tony and Academy Awards, and has had more than fifty Top-40 hits, including seven consecutive No. 1 U.S. albums, fifty-eight Billboard Top-40 singles, twenty-seven Top 10's, and nine No. 1's.

You might recognize Reginald Dwight by his other name—Elton John. What most people don't realize is that Elton John doesn't write his own lyrics. Except for two to three years in the late '70s when the team took a break from each other, Elton and his lyricist, Bernie Taupin, have worked together for almost fifty years.

Whenever I do a songwriting workshop I ask those present if they have ever heard of a man named Bernie Taupin. Often no one says yes, but every now and then one or two people may raise their hands. And yet, as Elton John's lyricist, Bernie Taupin gets 50 percent of all the royalties given to the songwriters. That's right. He and Elton John split the royalties fifty/fifty!

Some people hate not being recognized. They strut around hoping to catch someone's eye for the moment's pleasure of just being noticed. You can see this on the screen, on the football field, and in our normal day-to-day activities. Others, like Bernie Taupin, are okay with a life of hiddenness.

Maybe we should be a bit more like Bernie.

A LIFE LIVED IN THE SHADOWS

It needs to be said right off the bat that this chapter on the value of hiddenness was birthed from listening to a teaching given by a dear friend of mine, Bob Sorge. He shared about his life of hiddenness at a worship conference in Singapore we were at together in the early 2000s. He had been a successful worship leader and pastor when suddenly, after what should have been a routine surgery on his throat, something went wrong and he lost his voice completely. He could no longer sing and couldn't speak above a whisper. His life instantly and dramatically changed.

From the stage to the back room, hiddenness was thrust upon him. But unlike so many others, instead of thinking his purpose was over, Bob responded to the tragedy by pressing into God and finding out what was next. While still embracing the God who heals, Bob began to explore a new inner journey, and in so doing, he began to hear God like never before. Suddenly he found himself writing out his thoughts, page after page, and eventually authored one incredible book after another. By last count, he has written approximately twenty books, ranging topically from personal prayer, to worship, to envy, to the pain of perplexity and promotion. His story proved to me that a hidden life is not meant to be an inactive life.

A life of hiddenness is the ability to live in the shadows, no matter what life looks like. Sometimes it looks and feels painful or lonely. Other times there may be great favor, and yet we are able to make God shine brighter than ourselves. Volunteering to hide ourselves so that He shines the brightest is one of the greatest forms of hiddenness.

Let's see what hiddenness looks like in God's eyes. In Isaiah 49:2 it says,

> And He has made My mouth like a sharp sword;
> In the shadow of His hand He has hidden Me;
> And made Me a polished shaft;
> In His quiver He has hidden Me.

Many believe that this is a reference to Jesus and His time on earth. I agree, but I believe it also applies to each and every one of us. Jesus was a polished arrow for sure and He was hidden, so to speak, for thirty years before He officially began His ministry in earnest. He could have started earlier. He definitely was more than qualified. Yet He chose to wait until He received His release and His marching orders from His Father. If He knew how to walk in hiddenness, how much more is God calling us to embrace it as well?

Our modern culture has a superhero that did the same thing. A father "in the heavens" sends his son to earth where he is raised by a normal father and mother. He remains in the shadows, except for a brief moment, and after a time "away in the wilderness getting direction from his father," he returns to his world ready to walk out his call to bring justice and truth. It sounds like the story of Jesus—but it's not. It's Superman. The creators of *Superman*, two teenage Jewish boys named Jerry Siegel and Joel Shuster, were probably not thinking about Jesus when they wrote the initial story, but as they fleshed out the main character, they had to resolve a major plot difficulty: how it would be for Superman to know that he had tremendous power, yet to hide that power until it just the right time? Even superheroes need to learn how to live hidden lives.

It's just like the arrow from Isaiah 49:2. After the slow and painstaking job of making the finely shaped and useful arrow, it is polished, lifted up for inspection, and then gently placed in a dark and quiet quiver.

REACTIONS TO LIVING THE HIDDEN LIFE

Living a hidden life can be viewed from a number of different ways. To one person, that quiver feels protective and secure. It's a safe place until it's time to be used. To another, though, the quiver feels like a place of abandonment, confirming insecurities and one's sense of isolation and hopelessness.

Some think it means we take the road of John the Baptist when he said about Jesus in John 3:30, *"He must increase, but I must decrease."* I've heard many sermons and songs taken from this verse over the years. I used to think that it meant that I need to somehow make myself invisible so that only He can be seen. It sounds good. It even sounds extremely spiritual. "Oh, yes, God, hear my cry. Make me totally inconspicuous. Like a microscopic creature that no one even sees or notices when they pass by." But I believe now that this verse is about John realizing that his time (the time of the law and the prophets) was coming to an end and the new expression of God, His new covenant of grace, was about to come through Jesus. As Jesus said in Luke 16:16, "*The law and the prophets were until John. Since that time the kingdom of God has been preached, and everyone is pressing into it.*" John's proclamation of "decreasing" was about moving to a new age, from law to grace. It's not some kind of New Testament prayer about an invisibility cloak so that we can look and sound devoted.

If we choose to pull back and believe that we're called to "decrease," then we can come under the delusion that we are nothing and have nothing to give. But God's plan does not include us becoming invisible, otherwise He never would have said in Colossians 1:27 that He "*willed to make known what are the riches of the glory of this mystery among the Gentiles: which is Christ in you, the hope of glory.*" His desire is to make Himself great "in" us and "through" us. As 2 Corinthians 4:7 says, "*But we have this treasure in earthen vessels, that the excellence of the power may be of God and not of us.*" We don't glory in the earthen vessel, we glory in what's within. That said, earthen though we may be, He has chosen us to be *His*.

EXAMPLES OF HIDDENNESS

It's a paradox—that hiddenness to our eyes can actually be exalted recognition in God's. So let's take a step back and look at a couple of biblical characters who were men of great wisdom and strength, but were ushered into a life of hiddenness. A hidden life that made them great men.

JOSEPH

Joseph was a bit foolish when he shared his dreams with his brothers. "Hi guys, guess what? I had a couple of dreams where you will come before me and bow to me. Cool, huh?" Not the smartest move. That being said, his father didn't help him any. It says in Genesis 37 that his father loved Joseph more than all the others. He loved him so much that he made Joseph a tunic, or coat, of many colors. Just for Joseph, not his brothers. And in that time, "many colors" is code for "very, very expensive." Out of jealousy and frustration about this favoritism, his brothers hated him and could not find the grace to be kind or to speak peaceably to him.

I can just imagine what the atmosphere of the household was like—especially since we don't know how Joseph carried himself during that time. "Here I am, God, your man for the hour. I am such a finely polished arrow, so set me on your bow and let me fly. The world needs me. You'll be so glad You made me!"

So, just about then, God took that finely polished arrow and set him in His quiver. Into the dark place he went. I guess it wasn't so finely polished after all. For Joseph, his quiver experience was first a pit that his brothers threw him into and almost killed him. Then it was being sold as a slave, eventually ending up miles away in a rich guy named Potiphar's house.

It's amazing what a near-death experience at the hands of your brothers and being sold into slavery will do for a prideful heart. From this point on, there is no evidence of arrogance or pride being displayed in Joseph's life. It's just the opposite. When he is wrongly accused by Potiphar's wife of trying to take advantage of her, he takes another turn in God's quiver by being put into prison. But not just any prison. Because Potiphar was an officer of Pharaoh, Joseph was put into the prison where the king's prisoners were confined. Had Joseph not landed there he would not have been set up to go from the king's prison directly to the king. And that's exactly what he did. After many years of hiddenness, Joseph eventually found himself before the king, interpreting the king's dream. His next step was to be made the king's right hand man. His job…basically running the country. And in the best twist of fate ever, his brothers come to Egypt petitioning for food as a result of a terrible famine, and not knowing it's him, they bow before Joseph. Dream fulfilled!

If you look at Joseph's life, hiddenness did not define who he was or limit his use of his gifts. When sold as a slave to Potiphar, he didn't allow bitterness or rejection to dictate his actions. He humbled himself and began to serve, knowing that a man's gift makes room for him. Before long he became head of Potiphar's entire household. Hiddenness and humility will take you so much further than hiddenness and bitterness.

DAVID

David is another prime example of what happens when you're thrust into a hidden life. As we saw earlier, in chapter 2, David fell from a position of favor in Saul's eyes to the position of fugitive. In the blink of an eye, he went from a short but very visible stint as Saul's chosen one to a life in the shadows. In other words, David found himself in God's quiver. For the next season of his life, David was on the run, moving from town to town and cave to cave. It's known as David's Adullam years, named after a collection of caves near Jerusalem. Many scholars feel that this period of time lasted approximately eight years. *Eight long years* hidden away in God's quiver. Eight years that helped to shape a man who had a heart after God. Not a heart that *ran* after God so much as a heart that *took* after God.

I'm sure David would not have chosen that particular route to take in order to become king. None of us would. Interestingly, he had a chance to cut it short when Saul went into the same cave that David was hiding in and fell asleep. David's men tried to get David to kill Saul but David would have none of it. He would rather embrace his hidden life in God, and with it God's timetable, than force things by killing Saul himself. (See 1 Samuel 24.)

Saul's fight against David was birthed in jealousy and carried out while fighting an ever-increasing madness. David, on the contrary, had no fight against Saul. He would not lay his hand against one that he saw as *"the LORD's anointed"* (1 Samuel 24:6). That kind of integrity and revelation comes only through times of growth and maturing, times such as his years in God's quiver.

LACK OF HIDDENNESS

So why would I include a chapter on hiddenness when I have been encouraging everyone to step away from fear, rejection, and an assortment of other hindering baggage? The answer is actually very simple. My friend Bob Sorge said, "Promotion without pruning is like jumping into deep water without knowing how to swim." He went on, "Success can eat you alive, but reproach will keep you alive." What amazing wisdom! Of course, it's wisdom that has been gained through much pain.

However, it's important to differentiate between being hidden and being a victim. I know too many people who think that they are experiencing a hidden life because, for one reason or another, they have found themselves all alone. But detaching yourself from other people because of pain or hurt is not living a hidden life. Victims continue to blame others for their situation and rarely look closely or honestly at what brought about their circumstances. If they did, their world might fall apart. Little do they know that that's the best thing that could happen to them! They would get a whole new life with people waiting to embrace them with open arms.

In other words, hiddenness is not the same thing as hiding. If I'm hiding because I'm fearful of what would happen if I stepped into God's promises, I'm not experiencing hiddenness. I'm experiencing the results of fear. Outside influences didn't put me in that place, fear did, and I need to deal with the fear that keeps me in the dark, not in His shadow. People who embrace seasons of hiddenness are able to move away from a victim mentality and find God in the shadows.

VICTIMS CONTINUE TO BLAME OTHERS FOR THEIR SITUATION AND RARELY LOOK CLOSELY OR HONESTLY AT WHAT BROUGHT ABOUT THEIR CIRCUMSTANCES.

Can we be successful and yet be a person who lives in hiddenness? Absolutely! People do it all the time. It's because they don't equate their position from God as a position over men. Favor has a funny way of either changing a person or revealing what was there the whole time.

So what happens when increase and favor come your way and your heart is still swimming in the shallow end? Well, we see what happens all the time. Almost every day you hear news reports about someone whose giftings positioned them into a place of prominence, only to be brought down because of a lack of integrity and rectitude. It's a sad thing to see someone fall—and what's just as sad is to see that some take great pleasure in it.

That's one thing that I appreciate about the Word of God. Scripture doesn't sugarcoat things concerning the lives of biblical heroes or leaders. In fact, it is remarkably perspicuous as to men's success as well as their failures. Let's look at a couple of them to see how a life of hiddenness could have saved them.

SOLOMON

God came to Solomon face-to-face and promised him a future glory, just as He did to his father David. He only asked that Solomon keep his heart directed toward the Lord. As we all know, Solomon was the wisest and most rewarded man in history. First Kings gives us a quick history of his journey:

In 1 Kings 8, Solomon brings the Ark of the Covenant into the newly completed temple and restores it to its place in The Most Holy Place. That is followed by a time of worship that is so filled with the presence of God that the priests could no longer stand.

In 1 Kings 9, God appears to Solomon a second time, reminding him of His promises but also of Solomon's need to seek the one true God.

First Kings 10, Solomon becomes richer and is sought after by kings and queens around the known world. Even the Queen of Sheba seeks his great wisdom and marvels at his wealth.

In the rest of the book of 1 Kings, Solomon turns his heart away from God, first by his unchecked desires toward all his foreign wives and concubines and then by joining them in worshipping their false gods, even going as far as setting up high places for them to burn incense and sacrifice to their gods. God tears the kingdom from Solomon, only giving one tribe to his son for the sake of Solomon's father, King David. It's not even known if Solomon died as a follower of God or if he remained in the company of his wives and their gods.

It's amazing how smart people do such stupid things. It's even more amazing when the world's wisest man did the most stupid thing. Again, it's a good reminder that often, success can eat you but reproach will keep you.

UZZIAH

Then there was King Uzziah. Second Chronicles 26 gives us the outline of his rise to fame, his great favor with God and man, and his quick slide down into disease and despair.

In verse three, Uzziah is made king at the tender age of sixteen. He sought the Lord and was victorious against the Philistines. He built towns and fortified and protected the people. He was an inventor and equipped his army with new weapons. His fame spread far and wide and he was successful *until he became strong.*

Ah, there's that "famous and strong" thing again. It grabs people and does the strangest things. For Uzziah it had a terrible effect: *"But when he was strong his heart was lifted up, to his destruction, for he transgressed against the LORD his God"* (2 Chronicles 26:16). He decided that he was now qualified to burn incense just as if he were a priest. So that's exactly what he did. He entered the temple and began to burn incense. When the priests told him that he was out of order he became furious at them and in that instant he was struck with leprosy. Because of his leprosy he was banished to an isolated house, totally cut off from the house of the Lord. His son took over and Uzziah's reign as king came to an end.

OUR OWN DAY

And this didn't just happen in Bible times. Do any of these stories sound familiar?

+ The world's greatest biker wins the Tour de France year after year but, after denying for years that he used PEDs, he is outed and is banished from the sport he loves, losing the respect of the entire world and finding himself on the wrong end of a number of lawsuits.

❖ He is considered the greatest golfer in the modern era, but after a hidden life was exposed he took a mighty fall from grace, losing his marriage and the respect of much more than just the golf community. Though he was on his way to possibly breaking Jack Nicklaus' record of winning eighteen Majors, he has not won a Major Championship since.

❖ For years he was the face of a very popular sub sandwich company. His testimony of losing weight by eating their subs put him at the top of the advertising celebs. The slide from the top to the bottom happened quickly when it was revealed that he was engaging in illicit sexual conduct with minors. He is now serving his sentence in a federal correctional institution and is not eligible for release until July of 2029.

None of the previous stories was pleasant to write. These are people we all looked up to for one reason or another. They were using their gifts to the fullest, but unfortunately, like Uzziah, their hearts became *"lifted up."* Favor can be a trap if your heart is not in a good place. I want us all to fulfill our callings and potential, but often we come up short because the desire to be seen, to be great, or to be strong overwhelms the desire to hide ourselves in Him, which in the end, allows Him to be seen as great and strong.

How do we tell the difference between favor from man and favor from God? Well, sometimes it's both. Often, favor from God comes through the thoughts and decisions of men. It's easy to know the difference, though. One moves out of wisdom and moves toward something redeeming. The other has a hint of flattery, sometimes subtle, sometimes not so much. The end result of flattery is never good. In Job 17:5 it says that flattery brings about failure, even to the next generation. Daniel 11:32

says it even more strongly; it declares that flattery will bring about corruption to those who practice it.

Flattery's one goal is to lure you out from the shadow of His wings. Don't give in to it, no matter how great it feels and no matter how much you feel you need the boost. Let God be the one who promotes you.

FAVOR CAN BE A TRAP IF YOUR HEART IS NOT IN A GOOD PLACE.

David knew. He echoes it in Psalm 75:4–6 when he says, *"I warned the proud to cease their arrogance! I told the wicked to lower their insolent gaze and to stop being stubborn and proud. For promotion and power come from nowhere on earth, but only from God"* (TLB).

I love David's heart. It made no difference whether he was living in the midst of favor or experiencing the pain of failure. Either way, he made God his hiding place. In Psalm 17:8, he wrote, *"Hide me under the shadow of Your wings."* And in Psalm 32:7, he told the Lord, *"You are my hiding place."* There is no safer place to be than in His shadow.

As we grow and move in our individual strengths and gifts, may we always grow internally in our trust, our humility, and our ability to hide ourselves in Him. He is our hiding place. That's not a bad place to hang out. Just ask the arrows.

10

FALLING INTO GRACE

After his All Star baseball career was over, this former major league hero took an unlikely turn and found himself on Wall Street. He again became an all-star, managing a stock portfolio, and even writing a column for Jim Cramer's (host of CNBC's *Mad Money*) website. Soon thereafter, he started a magazine for former players called *Player's Club* and also started a high-end jet charter company. In 2006, his net worth was estimated to be around $50 million. By 2009, just three years later, he was living out of his car. That was the year an investigative article exposed his business failures, which included credit card fraud, failure to pay rent on the magazine's Park Avenue offices, and bounced checks. He filed for bankruptcy in 2009, both of his homes were foreclosed on, and a number of women accused him of sexual assault. He was arrested for grand theft auto,

cocaine possession, and identity theft. He was forced to sell his
World Series ring and he appeared in federal bankruptcy court,
charged with embezzlement, obstruction of justice, and bankruptcy fraud. On June 21, 2013, Lenny Dykstra, former Mets
and Phillies star, three-time All-Star and 1986 World Series
Champion was released from prison.

Almost daily (especially with our instant information from
social media) we hear one story after another of famous people
who, through a series of situations and choices, find themselves
in a horrible, and often very visible, fall from grace.

Often, they attribute it to one bad decision that they made.
"If only I hadn't done this," or "My real mistake was that." If
we're honest, though, lives that fall are never about one poor
decision. They're about a series of choices that people make,
sometime haphazardly, sometimes with forethought, but all
with the goal of benefitting themselves in one way or another.
What our culture never wants to say or imply is that often those
choices are morally wrong. Aka, sinful.

THE UNPOPULAR WORD

There, I said it. Sin. Our present-day Western mindset has
all but eliminated "sin" from our vocabulary. Instead, we use
phrases like, "poor decisions," or "unfortunate choices," or my
personal favorite, "a mistake." Please hear me. I'm not saying
that our poor decisions or mistakes are always sin. Not at all!
What I am saying is that if we use language to cover up what
is sin, we end up never actually dealing with the root of our
problem.

I'm a grace guy, so I can certainly understand what it means
to make poor decisions and poor choices. I can also say that
I've made more than my share of mistakes. What is necessary,
though, is to be able to truly understand what sin is, acknowledge

it, turn from it, and receive the wonderful forgiveness that only God can give. Without confession there is no forgiveness. Without forgiveness there is no freedom.

We all have sinned and we all have fallen short of the glory of God. Romans 3:23 is pretty clear about it. There isn't one person out there who hasn't sinned. Sometimes silently, sometimes not, sin piles up around us like waste and slowly begins to bring a stench to our lives. It also reshapes our brains. Just as grace begets grace and mercy begets mercy, so sin begets sin. It becomes a cycle, almost like an old merry-go-round. It seems easy and fun to get on, but over time, the merry-go-round moves faster and faster until it becomes almost impossible to jump off.

WITHOUT CONFESSION THERE IS NO FORGIVENESS. WITHOUT FORGIVENESS THERE IS NO FREEDOM.

Look at what the writer of Hebrews has to say about the effects of sin: *"Since we have such a huge crowd of men of faith watching us from the grandstands,* **let us strip off anything that slows us down or holds us back, and especially those sins that wrap themselves so tightly around our feet and trip us up;** *and let us run with patience the particular race that God has set before us"* (Hebrews 12:1 TLB).

Years ago, cigarette companies were required by the government to put warning labels on the side of their cigarette packs. They always sounded dire: "Smoking causes lung cancer, heart disease, and may complicate pregnancy." Or, "Quitting smoking now greatly reduces serious risks to your health." And my personal favorite that I once saw in an ad for a well-known brand: "Smoking can cause a slow and painful death." Yikes! Now, seriously, were people really surprised that smoking was bad for their health? I can't imagine someone buying a pack of cigarettes and saying to their friend, "Oh, my goodness, Billy Bob, it says right here that smoking isn't good for me. When did that happen?"

In the same way, we don't need a scary-sounding label to let us know that sin isn't our friend. And yet, the biggest reason we get stuck is because we can't deal with the sin problem in our lives. For anyone not trusting in Jesus for salvation, the sin problem is simply this: Has my sin been washed away through faith in the precious blood of Jesus or do I feel fine before "the heavens" because of the goodness of my lifestyle? If you're reading this book and you have not yet said "yes" to Jesus, you are missing out on the greatest gift a human being could have, that of being loved by the One who loves perfectly, of receiving that love, and of finding yourself invited into an eternal life of love. He's the only door to that eternal life and the only way to an internal peace.

NEW CREATION

If you do know Jesus and have a personal relationship with Him, sin is no longer your natural state. It was dealt with at the cross of Christ, once and forever. Does that mean that we never sin again? No—we still have a sin problem! We fall short of perfection again and again as we walk through life. But it does mean we are never in bondage to sin again because we can constantly run to Christ. Sin has lost its power. Because we are *"in Christ Jesus,"* there is *"therefore now no condemnation"* of us (Romans 8:1). The condemning power of sin was forever crushed at the cross. Even if we find ourselves struggling with sin and its devilish temptations, the eternal effects were nullified at the cross. YES!

To some, this understanding of God's grace sounds like a dream come true. Is it possible that God really dealt a death-blow to my sin? To others, this kind of grace sounds a little dangerous. Does that mean Christians can do whatever they want without any consequences? Paul, the writer of Romans, responds to both these vantage points. In Romans 6, Paul twice says, *"Shall we continue in sin that grace may abound?"* (Romans 6:1). The short answer is "no," but a simple "no" doesn't empower you. Paul understands that and addresses the real issue of the believer's identity: *"...do you not know that as many of us as were baptized into Christ Jesus were baptized into His death? Therefore we were buried with Him through baptism into death, that just as Christ was raised from the dead by the glory of the Father, even so we also should walk in newness of life"* (verses 3–4). Paul is addressing our new creation—not imposing a new form of legalism. We were buried with Him but now we've been raised with Him. In verse 18 he responds again with another level of our identity by saying that, *"...having been set free from sin, you became slaves of righteousness."* We have a new master. Sin has lost its power, and now grace *and* righteousness reign in our lives. Thanks be to God for His unfailing grace.

There is a movement within the church that would love to go back to living under the spirit of the Old Covenant laws. In fact, many don't believe that Jesus ushered in a New Covenant that replaced the Old Covenant. They believe that the New is now an addition to the Old. It's not so. Part of me can't comprehend this idea and yet I know for some, living by external rules (the love of law) is so much easier than living by an internal and ongoing relationship (the law of love).

What do I mean by "Old Covenant"? Well, first, let me emphatically say that the Old Testament is very different from the Old Covenant. The Old Testament is the inspired written Word of God. It has and will forever be God's Word, full of life and hope. Inside the Old Testament, we find descriptions and explanations of the Old Covenant, which was a temporary contract between God and man (originally Israel). The Old Covenant was for a purpose and a time but its purpose and time are over and it is now replaced by a new covenant made by Jesus at the cross. As He said at the Last Supper, *"This cup is the new covenant in My blood…"* (Luke 22:20). He was beginning a new covenant with man. To receive something new, you need to let go of something old. Again, I am not talking about letting go of God's Word (the Old Testament). But we do need to let go of the Old Covenant that God made with Moses and the people of Israel.

WITHOUT GOD COMING TO ME, I WOULD NEVER HAVE COME TO HIM.

Listen to what the writer of Hebrews says about the Old Covenant: *"For on the one hand there is an annulling of the former commandment because of its weakness and unprofitableness, for the law made nothing perfect; on the other hand, there is the bringing in of a better hope, through which we draw near to God"* (Hebrews 7:18–19). The law made nothing perfect. It was never meant to do that. It was meant to show us our need for a Savior. If we fall into sin and turn to some kind of law to save us, then we will forever be frustrated.

So what then, am I saying that sin is not really a problem? Not at all! Sin is THE problem. The thing is, Jesus came along and nailed the sin problem to the cross. Therefore, we have to believe that what He did is bigger than our sin. Our ability to even follow Him is contingent upon His grace to us. He is a better Leader than we are followers. He came to me with His prevenient grace (grace that came to me to awaken my heart) and showed me His mercy and truth, ushering me into His kingdom. Without God coming to me, I would never have come to Him.

Let me be very clear. Sin has consequences. We do reap what we have sown. Paul made that very clear. In Galatians 6:7–8, Paul says, "*Do not be deceived, God is not mocked; for whatever a man sows, that he will also reap. For he who sows to his flesh will of the flesh reap corruption, but he who sows to the Spirit will of the Spirit reap everlasting life.*" If I get caught for speeding, I will most likely get a ticket. If I get caught holding up a bank, I will end up with some pretty serious armed robbery charges. The great thing is that those who are in Christ Jesus have already sown to the Spirit and have within them the Spirit of God that moves the heart to continually sow to the Spirit. Yes we fall and fail, but grace will always prevail. Glory to God!

When I first thought about writing this particular chapter I was a bit hesitant. Often, people follow up with those things they focus on and I didn't want an entire chapter to be focused on sin. Then I remembered Paul's words in Galatians when he spoke *identity* instead of *consequences*. He understood that people need to see who they are so that they can become who they're called to be. If I see myself as a sinner I will inevitably give myself to that conceived reality. But if I realize that I *was* a sinner but that my sin has been washed and I am a loved son, I will begin to walk as a loved son, no longer making sin my priority or identity. Oh, I'll screw up but it will be the exception, not the rule, as in not that which rules over my life. I am a new creation!

Think of the new creation in terms of babyhood. A baby takes nine months to fully develop inside the womb, and yet it is growing every minute. It may take a while before it's actually born and seen, but huge amounts of growth are taking place. Natural laws are set in motion and that new baby continues to grow whether it knows it or not. It doesn't really participate in the growth. It has no choice in that growth. Yet, though it will take a long time to reach full maturity, that new life will grow. As I heard someone once say, "It's impossible not to grow."

Growth is not perfection. It's maturity. Sinless perfection will happen when we see Him face-to-face. Until then, like a newborn baby, you can't help but grow. Now that you're a believer, sin has a different affect upon you. It may tempt you but it cannot hold you. You're different. That's why sin bothers you. It's like the old story of the pig and the sheep. They may each fall into a muddy hole and they may each get covered in mud, looking very gross. The difference is, the pig loves the muddy hole and will wallow in it as long as he can. The sheep, on the other hand, will hate the feeling of being covered in mud and will get out as quickly as possible, and the next time he travels that way he will avoid the mud. The sheep has a different nature. In a similar way, all those who are in Christ Jesus may "fall in the mud," it is no longer their nature to stay there.

HOW GOD SEES US

Whenever a preacher goes down "sin lane," where the muddy holes await, they inevitably focus on the sins of famous biblical characters. The Old Testament seems to be the place that's easiest to stroll down. Adam and Eve had their bite and changed everything. Cain committed the first murder (my, that didn't take long). Moses struck the rock and was barred from entering the Promised Land. Major bummer! Saul improperly sacrificed by taking on the role of a priest and in so doing his family lost the heritage of his kingdom. The list goes on and on.

Yes, and then there's David, a man after God's own heart. Even David had his sinful side. He was an adulterer and a murderer. So what saved him? Well, he did reap division within his household that forever changed the future of his kingdom, but he himself found peace with God. How? Look again at the description of David. He was a man "after" God's own heart. Not the definition of *after* that an athlete would understand, such as "running after." (Imagine if that's what God meant. If that were the case we would all be most miserable. None of us are fast enough to catch God!) Rather, for David, it was the definition of one who "takes after" another, such as a son who takes after his father. David understood the heart of God, and, as a result, he carried the capacity to feel how God felt. Therefore, when he was confronted with his detestable sin, he threw himself at God's feet, relying on his knowledge of God's mercy and grace.

If we would only know how God sees us and how He feels about us we would never try to run from Him. I learned years ago a good barometer of whether I truly see God as One who is full of grace and mercy. It's simply this: when I fall or fail, do I run toward Him or do I run away from Him? The first tells me that I really do understand His grace and the second reminds me that I'm still not seeing who He really is and what He's really like. This I do know: He is always better that we can ever imagine!

Let your focus be on who God says you are. Listen to what He says about you:

You are complete in Him. (See Colossians 2:10.)

You are free from the law of sin and death. (See Romans 8:2.)

You are holy and without blame before Him in love. (See Ephesians 1:4 and 1 Peter 1:16.)

You have the greater One living in you; for greater is He who is in you than he who is in the world. (See 1 John 4:4.)

You have received the gift of righteousness and reign as a king in life by Jesus Christ. (See Romans 5:17.)

You show forth the praises of God who has called you out of darkness into His marvelous light. (See 1 Peter 2:9.)

You are God's child, born again of the incorruptible seed of the Word of God, which lives and abides forever. (See 1 Peter 1:23.)

You are God's workmanship, created in Christ unto good works. (See Ephesians 2:10.)

You are a new creature in Christ. (See 2 Corinthians 5:17.)

You are a partaker of His divine nature. (See 2 Peter 1:3–4.)

You are the righteousness of God in Jesus Christ. (See 2 Corinthians 5:21.)

You are the temple of the Holy Spirit. (See 1 Corinthians 6:19.)

You have been forgiven of all your sins and are washed in the blood. (See Ephesians 1:7.)

You are delivered from the power of darkness and translated into God's kingdom. (See Colossians 1:13.)

You are redeemed from the curse of sin. (See Galatians 3:13.)

You are greatly and perfectly loved by God. (See Romans 1:7; Ephesians 2:4; Colossians 3:12.)

You have an identity as a loved son or daughter. If you're in Christ you're no longer a sinner. Somehow there seems to be a mindset that if we say *we are* sinners saved by grace we are expressing some form of spiritual humility. We're not. Humility mixed with untruth is still untruth. I *was* a sinner saved by grace but that is a former title. I am now His own, He in me and I in Him. It's all about identity. Don't make sin, in any form, part of your identity. Make Him your focus and then make what He says about you your identity.

YOUR HEART'S DESIRE

Is the reason you feel stuck because you don't feel worthy of your dream? Is it because you haven't fully absorbed your new identity in Him? God Himself doesn't want a robot army of followers. He wants you—your unique self, your unique dream. Because He wants you to be *unstuck*, no power in the world can keep you in the quagmire of unfulfilled purpose. My prayer for you is the prayer of Psalm 20:4: *"May He grant you according to your heart's desire, and fulfill all your purpose."* Amen.

EPILOGUE

Two last points…ok, yeah, three.

First, getting stuck is a part of life. No one is immune from it. Somehow, many twentieth- and twenty-first-century believers have gotten the idea that our lives as believers should be pain-free. They feel such great disappointment in themselves and in God when confronted with the many obstacles that come to us in life.

Jesus said in Matthew 5 that His Father sends rain on the just and on the unjust. The last few days where I am it has been raining almost nonstop. And every believer I know has actually had to go out in the same rain as the most hard-hearted unbeliever. Natural rain, as well as natural obstacles, come our way daily.

What we need to understand, though, is the difference between natural rain and an oppressive fire hose. The enemy of our souls wants to douse our fire and render us, if not lifeless, then at least passive. I'm a mellow guy but a life of passivity is not what I signed up for. Jesus came to give us life, and life abundantly.

Fear, rejection, pride, sin, etc., are not natural rains from God. Each of these is an unnatural rain, a false rain sent to discourage us. Each one lies to us about ourselves and about Him. God hasn't given us the spirit of fear, but of power, love, and soundness of mind. He will never leave us not forsake us. Though we may feel separate from Him, we never are. He is faithful to His Word.

If His gifts and callings are without repentance, meaning that He will never withdraw them from our lives, can we see that what we have been given by God must be important to us and to Him? Otherwise, He would have made sure that if we were not always faithful, those gifts would vanish like a vapor. But He didn't do that. Therefore, what I hold and possess from Him is most precious and I need to press through and learn to run the hurdles through till the end. You can't go over hurdles when you're low. You need to be lifted up.

Second, when I do finally scale that cliff, get through that downpour, conquer that attack, and gloriously pass over that last hurdle, what's next? Look at 2 Corinthians 1:3–4: *"Blessed be the God and Father of our Lord Jesus Christ, the Father of mercies and God of all comfort, who comforts us in all our tribulation, that we may be able to comfort those who are in any trouble, with the comfort with which we ourselves are comforted by God."*

My gifts were never meant to end with me. They were meant to flow from me. My tribulations were not meant just to test me, they were opportunities for me to become equipped.

It's an amazing thing to watch people overcome the barriers and stumbling blocks in their lives, but it takes on a special beauty when that same person turns that experience into a gift of grace for the next person.

Now, there's a difference between being a comfort to another by our actions and our words and becoming a boastful and portentous teacher to others because of our varied experiences. People don't want to hear, "This is what you should do..." or "When I was in your shoes..." or the beloved phrase, "I told you so." They want to know that we care and that because of our background and past history, we have compassion. People can hear almost anything when they see your compassion and know that you really do care. Without compassion, we become detached teachers of truth instead of empathetic and present comforters. May the comfort that God and others have brought to us equip us with a kindness and compassion that enables us to become a wellspring of comfort to those around us.

> WITHOUT COMPASSION, WE BECOME DETACHED TEACHERS OF TRUTH INSTEAD OF EMPATHETIC AND PRESENT COMFORTERS.

Third, and last, but most certainly not least, the purpose of my life has never been about the fulfillment of my heart's desires or the full release of my gifts. It's simply about the glorification of God. I am here to bring glory to God with my life. If I become the center of my life, I miss the purpose of my life.

This book is meant to be an encouragement to those who feel *stuck* in one thing or another doing this thing we call life. When we absorb the fact that we are here for a purpose, it adds an extra weight and relevance to who we are and what we do every day. What it's not meant to do is create an overemphasis on the importance of "me." Yes, for the joy set before Him He endured the cross. And yes, I was that joy. I was that purpose for His leaving heaven and coming to bring salvation to man. But, behind that purpose is a greater one. In *The Lion, the Witch, and the Wardrobe* by C. S. Lewis, there is a scene when Aslan has been raised from the dead. The young girls, Susan and Lucy, are ecstatic but they can't understand how he can be alive. They talk of the deep magic that the witch knew that led him to his death. Aslan agrees with them but tells them that the witch didn't know about the deeper magic—a deeper truth that she never knew.

So it is with our lives. We look to uncover the "magic" of our lives, which is a noble thing. However, there is a deeper purpose in each of us that yearns to discover our identity and craves to fulfill our destiny. We think it's about us but it really isn't. I was not made for me. I am here for Him. I was made "for His pleasure."

When that reality hits us it allows us to become a conduit for His life to flow through us. Without that knowledge, who we are and what we do will end up drawing attention to ourselves, and honestly, no one has the power to bring about abundant life, divine healing, forgiveness of sin, the removal of guilt and shame, and the glory of redemption and the promise of everlasting life. That's His territory!

Whatever you're stuck in right now, take courage: you can overcome. Whether you are able to jump up and start running, to plod steadily forward, or just slowly put one foot in front of the other through the mud, remind yourself that you were meant to be on the move. Stuck spots may slow you down a bit, but remember, you were made to get up and keep moving. May this book help you do that!

ACKNOWLEDGMENTS

A big hearty thank you to my friend and editor Don Milam. Don, you're more than a voice on the other end of the phone. You're a faithful man of God, who, in spite of some of life's most difficult obstacles, pressed into God and, as a result, continue to give life to those around you.

To Christine Whitaker of Whitaker House. Thank you for believing that I had more books in me. Your graciousness is appreciated. I pray that it's also richly rewarded.

To Judith Dinsmore, lead editor extraordinaire from Whitaker House. You are amazing! You have an ability to take the ordinary and create the extraordinary. Thank you for your relevant input and your wise suggestions. I'm happy to have your eyes and heart on anything I write.